Samon

# from defeat to Victory

Samone Yancy

Samone Yancy

Copyright © 2013 Samone Yancy

All rights reserved.

ISBN:0615813240
ISBN-13: 978-0615813240

## DEDICATION

First and foremost I thank my Lord and Savior Jesus Christ for getting my life to this point, I am eternally grateful.

To My husband Clarence Yancy Jr., words could never explain the agape love I have for you. You are my world and my everything. I am enjoying this journey with you!

To my boys Marquise and Mykell, because of you two I made the best decision I could have ever made (besides marrying your daddy) selling out to God. I do what I do for the both of you. Mommy loves you!

Samone Yancy

# CONTENTS

Acknowledgments
Introduction

| | | |
|---|---|---|
| 1 | Victory over your Flesh | 1 |
| 2 | Victory over your Spiritual Walk | 29 |
| 3 | Victory over your Daily Walk | 43 |
| 4 | Victory in your Relationships | 53 |
| 5 | Victory in your Home(Married) | 62 |
| 6 | Victory in your Home(Singles) | 73 |
| 7 | Victory on your Job | 80 |
| 8 | Victory over your Finances | 87 |

Samone Yancy

Samone Yancy

## ACKNOWLEDGMENTS

To my son and daughter Terrence and Ca'Nia Yancy- thank you for sharing your dad with me, I love you both!

To my mom Ann Logan, I thank you and love you. Because of you I grew up with nothing but the best. As a little girl I never knew you were so young raising me, but you were. I know it was not always easy and I gave you plenty of challenges. But look at the woman I am today. But God!

To my dad Mark Logan, I thank God for you. You have always been there for me. Because of you I know what a real provider is. Because of you I never had to seek love and affection from a man. You have been an exceptional father.

To my biological dad Sammie Estell Jr.(Maria). As I conclude this book of my spiritual journey, only the most High God could've brought you into my life at this time. I am soo thankful!

To my mother-in-law Robbie Thomas(Papa Charles), thank you, for accepting me as your daughter and always going above and beyond. I could not have asked for a better grandmother to my boys.

To my father-in-law"pa-pa Michigan" (Grandma Joyce), thank you for being there, accepting me, and loving me as your daughter. You are a great pa-pa…all the way from Michigan!

To my sisters, Tiffani and Nia, I love y'all and pray for you all the time. I'm always here for the both of you. And to my nephew Christian! One day you will be able to read this.

To my stepsister Danyell, my nieces, and nephew, Love you all!

To my sister-in-law Andria"Puddin" Yancy, and my nephews, Love you all!

To my grandfather, grandmother, aunts, uncles, cousins, on both sides of the family. Rest in Peace to my grandmother Minnie, uncle Rickey, Lil Mark, Lil Sam, and all my loved ones that have left this earth.

To my cousin Chrissie Appleby, thank you! You took this journey with me and were there when no one else was. I will always appreciate you and the bond we have. Love you cousin!

To my Ark of Safety church family. Special shout out to Spiritual Counseling and Teen Ministry.

To my Pastor, Raymond Horry and First lady Minister Kathy Horry I deeply appreciate your obedience. Words could never express how much of a blessing the two of you have been to my family. So many seeds have been planted into my life under your leadership. You taught me authority and submission, how to be a woman, wife, and mother. For that I am eternally grateful.

To my CWWIV girls I thank you, for following my leadership, and trusting and believing in me. The best is yet to come for all of us!!

To Nicole Powell, my sis and BFF ...YOU ALREADY KNOW! LOL

To my assistant and friend, Nakesa Green, I thank you. You are a TRUE SERVANT, I appreciate you more than you know!

To Mom Hilda "H" Hobbs, thanks for editing and fixing my broken English! Your timing was perfect!

To Pastor Eric Battle my brother in Christ, thanks for helping me along the way. Because of you I was able to get started with this book. Thanks for all of the meetings, phone calls, and text messages.

To Author Tiffany Nicole Woods, thank you for creating my beautiful book cover! You are true "Godnection!"

Samone Yancy

# INTRODUCTION

"Lord, why are so many Christian women struggling in their walk with You?" I asked God this simple question. His response gave birth to this book and started me on my own personal Spiritual Journey with Him.

The Lord spoke to me, "It is time for Believing women to let go of everything that's keeping them from loving Me with their whole being: mind, body and soul. It's time for Believing women to be free from depression, low self-esteem, insecurities, obesity, meaningless relationships, friendships, bad attitudes, fear, discouragement and doubt. Anything that does not glorify Me or bring them closer to Me, now's time to let it go."

After God spoke and I received, He made my spiritual eyes and ears sensitive to my own personal struggles, as well as, the struggles of other Believing women. This was the point in my life where I moved from BELIEVING in God to LIVING for God. I know, with all that is in me, God graced me to go through trials and tests, so I would have a testimony to help other women in their struggles.

How seriously do you want a real and personal relationship with God? How seriously do you want to fulfill His Purpose? Hopefully, enough to allow Him to clean up your life, so that you can begin to glorify Him in every area and to stop believing the enemy's lies that this is as good as your life will get or that you don't deserve a blessed life. The devil's job will always be to kill, steal and destroy the Plan and Purpose God has for our lives. He knows as long as we are depressed, stressed, and caught up in people and things that do not add value to our lives, we will never fulfill our purpose. Reaching back, I remember how I let the enemy take me to some dark places. He consumed my mind with thoughts of suicide, because my life was not what I had envisioned; but in reality, my life was what it was because of the choices I made coming out of high school. The devil had me exactly where he wanted me, feeling hopeless and depressed.

Your thoughts, even attempting suicide, are one of the biggest tricks of the enemy; he would like nothing more than to see you take yourself out. He reminds us of our failures and disappointments, so we will continue to be discouraged. There is nothing worse than feeling like a failure. The enemy will use this to hold you captive in your own mind, trying to keep you in that dark place and making you feel it's impossible to get out. Know and believe you are reading this book because God is real. He loves you; He cares about you and your situation; He understands you; He is very interested in you. The very situation you are going through right now, God knows all about it. The prayers you don't think he hears, He does; and at this very moment, He is working it all out.

*"Give all your worries to Him, because He cares about you."* 1 Peter 5:7

As you read this book, I pray your spirit is sensitive to the Voice of God. My Pastor, Raymond D. Horry, says all the time "God cannot be explained, He has to be experienced." This book, inspired by my Heavenly Father, is not to teach about or explain God; it is me sharing with you some of my experiences with Him.

It is me taking you on my personal journey from defeat to VICTORY. The purpose is to let every Believing woman, who is struggling in her relationship with God, know she has the victory in Christ Jesus.

If you truly desire to draw closer to Him, you will. It will come with instructions, but know every instruction is a test. Every test you pass will draw you closer to Him. He might tell you to get out of a relationship or let go of some friendships; this is for your own good. The closer you get to Him, the more you will understand how deep God's Love is for you. I pray, with this understanding, you will begin to be healed emotionally and physically. You will be changed and delivered from everything and everyone who has a hold on you. I pray you see yourself as the woman God created you to be. I bind, in the name of Jesus, the spirit of depression, bitterness, doubt, fear, discouragement, loneliness and any other spirit not of God. I pray, when you finish this book, you will be confident like never before. Receive God's Love and be blessed. You have the VICTORY!

## A Call to VICTORY (receive Christ)

**Victory** - a success or triumph over an enemy in battle or war.

The victory I am speaking of, throughout this entire book, is the victory only obtainable through a relationship with Jesus Christ. 1Corinthians 15:57 states, *"But we thank God! He gives us the victory through our Lord Jesus Christ."*

If you have never invited Jesus Christ into your heart, I pray you receive him right now.

The Word of God tells us, *"If you use your mouth to say, 'Jesus is Lord,' and you believe in your heart that God raised Jesus from the dead, you will be saved."* Romans 10:9

Whether facing a battle of the mind, health or body, Satan is the driving force behind it. His main priority is to destroy our souls and keep us away from the Kingdom of God. The enemy will fill your head with lies: "That's just the way you are. You can never change. You will never be healed. You will never find love. You are ugly. You are fat. You are a bad person." He will try to put all of these lies in your mind; he is a liar, the master of lies; there is no truth in him.

The devil's objective is to get to the Heart of God, and the only way to do so is to mess with his children. It's really not about us; he has no interest in us, but he understands the love God has for His children. Imagine trying to please a man; only to discover, he has no interest in you at all! This is enough to make me say, "Get to steppin' devil!!"

Without a doubt, there is a man who loves us; His name is Jesus Christ. I pray you have invited Him into to your heart, so He can be the Head of your life.

Confess right now:
Lord, I invite you into my heart, and I ask you to forgive me for my sins. I acknowledge you are God, and you are in total control. Lord, I ask you to lead and direct my life; let Your Will be done, in Jesus' name. Amen!

## Chapter 1 - Victory over the Flesh

### What is the Flesh?

Only the flesh gets lonely and depressed, craves cigarettes, smokes weed, uses drugs, drinks and gambles. Not one of these desires comes from the spirit. The flesh deals with the human body and its weaknesses, including the mind, attitude, and emotion. The flesh always desires instant gratification and fights against the spirit daily. Your flesh might be trying to keep you from reading this book right now, but keep reading! We have to purpose in our hearts to keep the flesh in check; if not, it will always overrule our spirit.

All of our issues, struggles or addictions are tied to the flesh. We must learn to monitor ourselves daily; think about why we do the things we do, why we feel the way we feel. When we recognize our pattern of behavior, we can, then, do something about it. This process is necessary; because once we say, "Yes," to Jesus, we are automatically signed up for spiritual warfare. The spirit is now alive, and the flesh is fighting to stay in control. In order to gain victory, we have to recognize we are in a spiritual warfare; Satan is our enemy, but Jesus is our VICTORY. He is the one who fights our battles; we can never defeat the enemy in our own strength. God tells us in His Word to,

*"Walk in the Spirit and we will not fulfill the lust of the flesh."*

Galatians 5:16

The Spirit of the Lord wants us, Believing women of God, to know we are dying (spiritually) as we cater to our flesh (our sinful nature). The enemy has tricked us into thinking when we get married, have kids, get a house, a job, or reach a certain financial status then, our life will be worth living. This is the biggest lie from the enemy. We must seek first His Kingdom and His Righteousness and develop a relationship with Him.

*"Seek ye first the kingdom of God and his righteousness and all these other things shall be added unto you."* Matthew 6:33

But, we are not TRULY seeking God first; we are seeking things and people without any input from God. We are trying to fill the void in our life only He can fill. We are replacing a space reserved only for God with temporary things and people. God's fulfillment is everlasting, not temporary.

Most of us are struggling in our flesh as a result of past mistakes. We have allowed these mistakes to affect our emotions, self esteem and trust level.
Then, once we become Believers, we wonder why we are struggling in our walk with God. We fail to see we are bringing our past worldly mindset into the Kingdom. We are bringing all of this baggage: neediness, lack of trust, and fear into our new life. We have to understand the Word is true.

*"Therefore, if anyone is in Christ, he is a new creation; the old has gone, the new has come!"*
2 Corinthians 5:17
After accepting Christ, our spirit man who was lying dormant, is now alive. In the world, our flesh was automatically in control, now that we have accepted Christ, our spirits are in control. Of course, we do not automatically know how to obey our spirits; it is a process. We learn to obey our spirits as we tell our flesh "No." The more we do not let our flesh control us, the more power we give to the spirit and the more grace we receive. When I began writing this book, I asked a number of Believing women to share

their struggles of the flesh, in their own words:

- "I'm thinking fear."
- "Depression and trying to prove to others that I'm okay, when really I'm not."
- "I struggle with fear! I struggle with life and death. The fact that I don't know when, and or how I'll leave this earth has me fearful."
- "It takes great strength to get my flesh to say no to people."
- "For me, I struggled with doubt."
- "My struggle was my attitude due to life not turning out as planned."
- "I was fondled at a very young age by a teenage boy while I was asleep. My mother caught him and told me what happened. My body experienced something that my mind does not remember. I believe this experience caused my body to crave that touch which led me to having sex at an early age. Even though I became wiser, as I got older, my body still craved sex."

Even from this small percentage of women, we see that issues arise due to a number of reasons. When operating in the flesh and experiencing any one of the above issues without God, we seek other people and things to help us with our fears, doubts, sexual desires and attitudes toward life. And when those people or the things don't work out; we get depressed and angry. This occurs when we put our hope and trust in anything other than God. We must learn to trust that God will take care of us and provide all we need, mentally and physically. The enemy will always use our fears, insecurities and weaknesses to hinder the plans God has for our lives.

During our teen years, we have dreams and goals. We clearly see the life we want to live. I believe, these innocent dreams and desires come from God; but immediately after, if we are not purposing to live for God, the enemy comes right in and destroys our God given dreams. I know I am not the only one whose life turned into something far from what I envisioned. We all had big plans for our future.

Some of us got caught up in relationships with the wrong crowd of people, perhaps leading to pregnancy, drugs, drinking, illicit lifestyles or even becoming people pleasers. We pick up the spirit of laziness and procrastination. This is all from the enemy. He doesn't care that we're young with no life experience. He comes to kill, steal and destroy the plan God has before it even begins. We all have a root cause to our problem, something or someone who influenced us.

Maybe you have not, yet, recognized yourself. If that's the case, I urge you to pray and ask God to show you right now why you feel or act the way you do. When He does reveal why, receive it and allow Him to help you. Ask Him to show you why you keep making the same bad decisions, choosing the wrong people to hang around. What void are you trying to fill?

Others probably would not believe how unhappy, how depressed you are with your life, because you never show it. That was me. For a long time, I was mad at myself for not going to college, mad at how my life was turning out. So many times I contemplated suicide, because I could not see my life any better. If any of you have attempted, or even thought about, suicide, you must know this is one of the biggest tricks of the enemy! God has plans for you and your life; never let the enemy tell you your life is over or you messed up too badly. Every day you wake up, the devil is defeated; and if for no other reason, you have to praise God for that.

We all deal with our failures differently. I thank God I have never experimented with hard drugs; but this doesn't make me better than a drug addict, because my addictions were something else: I was addicted to gambling; I was sexually active at an early age; I hung around the wrong people. I picked up my gambling addiction hanging out with one of my friends. At 18, I was shooting craps and playing black jack. At first, it was just for fun; then, it became a comfort, almost like an escape from the world. Sometimes I would go to two or three gambling boats in a night; the devil really had me! It was another one of his tricks to keep me depressed, broke and without hope; and for a few years, he was winning. So many times I would ride home in tears, because I gambled away all of my money.

I'm speaking to somebody. You are that person no one would ever suspect; you appear to have all of your stuff together; but in reality, you can't even pay your bills. Sometimes, you have to sleep around to keep your lights on; I know I'm not the only one. God is trying to set you free!!! I think back now, and I just cannot believe who I was. I pray, right now, for every woman struggling with that gambling demon; I call you delivered right now in Jesus' name!! You can find other things to do rather than gamble your money away. There are things in our lives we can all say we regret or wish we would have done better or different, but do not let regrets keep you from moving forward. As long as you are living, it's never too late.

## Generational Curses

Many of us are dealing with inherited sins, those passed down from our parents (generational curses). I do believe in generational curses; it is more a struggle of the mind. A curse is not who you are, it is not final. With prayer and the renewal of your mind, it can be broken. When I think of generational curses, my mind goes back to the Garden of Eden. Because of the sin of Adam, sin fell upon all mankind.

*"Therefore just as sin entered the world through one man, and death through sin, and in this way death came to all men, because all sinned."* Romans 5:12

We do not serve a mean and cruel God, but we do serve a God who stands by His Word.

*"God is not a man, that he should lie, nor the son of man, that he should change his mind."* James 23:19

Some people have a hard time accepting God, because they want to question, "If God is good, then why do bad things happen? Why do babies die?" Why do we have earthquakes, tsunamis and tornadoes?" The answer is because of the sin that is in this world.

From the beginning, God told Adam, *"...but you must not eat from the tree of knowledge of good and evil, for when you eat of it you will surely die."* Genesis 2:17

Because God spoke this, He is obligated to keep His Word. When God said Adam would die, he did not mean physical death; he was talking about spiritual death. Adam did not die (spiritually) because God is mean; he died because God always keeps His Word. Sin causes death. Every time we sin, something in our lives dies; it could be death in our finances, our marriage, our mind, our body or in the lives of our children. We have to understand how much God hates sin, not the people but the acts of sin the people commit.

The Good News is that the same God who cannot lie is, also, a God who is faithful and merciful. Sin came into the world through Adam, but our faithful God sent us a Second Adam, the Savior of the World, Jesus Christ. He came into the world to save us (those who believe in Him) from our sins. Don't get caught up in the First Adam, thinking how we could serve such a cruel God; come to know the Second Adam, the Savior of the World, come to know the faithfulness of our God. The God who keeps His Word in the bad times is the same God who keeps His Word in the good times. This is exciting; God is the only one who will ALWAYS keep His Word. He is not like man, fickle and changes his mind; He is a God who keeps His Promises. The same way sin fell upon us through Adam is the same way sin has come upon us through our parents; it was not the Will of God in the garden, and it's not the Will of God in our lives today.

The Lord spoke to me about today's generational curses. There was a time when all we had were praying grandmothers and even if our parents didn't take us to church, our grandmother did. They sowed in us to love and trust God, even if they never said it. We knew by the peaceful lives they lived, the songs they sang, they hymns they hummed. I thank God I was able to experience having two grandmothers who took me to church. Every Sunday, I remember my great grandmother's house full of people from church. There was food, freshly baked peach cobbler, sweet potato pies, and the kids' favorite, popcorn balls! I wonder where she got the money to feed everybody, when they were barely making ends meet. Now, I know it was simply because she was faithful to God, to the church, to paying bills and was not caught up in keeping up with the Jones. They were satisfied and content with life. Our grandmothers had real experiences with the Lord, and they knew him to be faithful. Only God's grace could have gotten them through slavery and hard living. Once you truly experience God, people will begin to question your peace; they will wonder why you are not losing your mind going through difficult situations.

As a newborn, the enemy tried to cut my life short. I was diagnosed with a tumor in my nose, but these praying grandmothers took me to the altar. It is the prayers of these women that make it possible for me to write about our God; they covered me in prayer from the time I was a baby. I know I am an example of God's faithfulness to them and even to the grandmothers I never had a chance to know. I can sense their spirits and know they are watching me saying, "God Is Faithful!" Recently, one of my aunts shared with me, "Your great-great grandmother was truly a praying woman." This really blessed my soul and encouraged me. Because of these women and with the help of my own will and yielding to the Spirit, God is using me in a mighty big way.

The prayers of the past grandmothers are wearing off; we are losing our covering. God is looking for those who will take a stand for righteousness and holiness in their families. We need to keep our children covered. Instead of mothers and grandmothers praying for their children, they are now partying with them, living in just as much sin as their children. Today's mothers are grandparents before they reach forty. The number of mothers and grandmothers strung out on drugs and practicing lesbian lifestyles has increased. Our covering is wearing off, and God desires to bring it back; not exactly the same as it was, because we are in a different dispensation, but He is calling us, Women of God, to take our rightful places in order to show this younger generation what having a relationship with God can do.

Sin is on the increase. Instead of partying with our kids, we should be praying for them and living a righteous lifestyle before them. This is a "show me" generation. What good are prayers for our children, if we are not living a lifestyle pleasing to God? We have to repent and turn from our evil ways; only then, will God move on our behalf. It is not possible to raise perfect children, but we have to plant the seeds in them. We must show them we practice what we preach, so when they are older and experiencing the world first hand, they will come back to all we have taught and placed on the inside of them. They will remember what they saw and heard (negative or positive). We are the first influence in our children lives. How can we think it is okay to party, drink, smoke or engage in sinful acts with or around our children? We wonder why our lives are cursed. How can they respect others when they are not taught that at home? When our children become parents, chances are high they will raise their children in the same sinful way. When does the cycle end?

God is talking to those who claim to know Him, those who have confessed Jesus is Lord. God is not surprised by the condition of the world, but He expects more out of us Believers. There are no excuses, whatever negative things you don't like about your mother, father, family or whoever else, make a decision to do the opposite. It is not who you are any longer. Stop telling yourself because your mother dealt with depression, you will deal with depression; because your father was an alcoholic, you will be one. The cycle will only end when someone recognizes this as a curse and lets God use them to break the cycle. All God needs is one person who is willing to take a stand. I am sensing, in my spirit, you are that one person in your family, with the help of God, who can make a difference.

Families with the curses of cancer, high blood pressure, diabetes, aids, drugs, homosexuality and alcohol are fighting spirits of the devil. They have no power or control, unless you give it to them. Let God speak in all of this. We break these spirits with prayer and righteousness, but praying alone is not good enough. You must live a lifestyle pleasing and acceptable.

*"...The prayer of a righteous man is powerful and effective."*
James 5:16

If prayers over your family are not being answered, maybe you need to look at your own lifestyle. Yes, it is a person's own will, but you cannot look at someone and know what's in the heart. The alcoholic, the drug addict, we cannot judge whether or not they want to be delivered. Maybe it's your prayer that will help God deliver them. We have to get in the spirit and get rid of our carnal minds.

*The Lord does not look at the things man looks at. Man looks at the outward appearance, but the Lord looks at the heart.* 1Samuel 16:7

We are in an age where so much knowledge and power are available to us, and it's time to tap into it. Stop accepting things as, "That's just the way it is." God is looking for just one person in your family to take a stand. Be that one, through prayer and righteous living, whom God uses to break every generational curse, every strong hold that has your family bound. Let God use you in a mighty way.

## How to Control the Flesh

As women of the Most High God, we have been given authority, power, and dominion. In the beginning, God said,

*Let us make man in our own image, in our likeness, and let them rule over the fish of the sea and the birds of the air, over the livestock, over all the earth, and over all the creatures that move along the ground.* Genesis 1:26

Not only did He give us rule over all the creatures in the earth, He also gave us,

*...the authority to trample on snakes and scorpions and to overcome all the power of the enemy.* Luke10:19

Thus, we have power over our minds, bodies and attitudes; but how do we operate in that power? Prayerfully, you have acknowledged God as the Father, Son and the Holy Spirit; and you have been filled with His Spirit.
The Holy Spirit is our helper,

*But the Counselor, the Holy Spirit, whom the Father will send in my name, will teach you all things and will remind you of everything I have said to you.* John 14:26

Apart from God we can do nothing, but with him all things are possible. (Philippians 4:13) There is no way we can gain the victory God promised us in His Word without the help of the Holy Spirit. If you are a believer, but have never invited the Holy Spirit to dwell on the inside of you and yet, have the desire to go higher; please, take time to invite Him in right now, "Lord fill me with your Spirit."

*"If you then, though you are evil, know how to give good gifts to your children, how much more will your Father in Heaven give the Holy Spirit to those who ask him?"* Luke 11:13

The Holy Spirit is the power every Believer needs. You can still be saved without the Holy Spirit, but there is no way you can be all God created you to be without being filled with His Spirit. After you have been filled, nothing will be impossible for you.

*Now to Him who is able to do immeasurably more than all we ask or imagine, according to his power that is at work within us.* Ephesians 3:20

Remember, the Holy Spirit helps us, but we definitely must do our part. First, we must recognize our struggles of the flesh so we can confess them to God and allow Him to come in. We begin forming a relationship with God as we learn to talk and be real with Him. He already knows about every struggle and situation, but we have to be able to acknowledge them and then, find out what the Word of God says concerning our situation.

Begin to confess the Word out loud; this gives God, our Father, an invitation to come in and help us. We are making ourselves partners with God. He wants us to be active in our deliverance. He will not just take the taste from your mouth, if you are an alcoholic or take away your sexual desires, if you are a fornicator. You have to go through, so you can come out and give God the Glory. We come to God with so much baggage and expect Him to just fix it. We receive Salvation because of the mercy of God; He comes to our rescue only to help us with our mess. He sees and knows everything we are going through.

God wants us to rely on Him and Him alone. So many of us women, in this generation, feel we have to be validated by a man, or we take the opposite extreme and act as if we don't need anyone. The latter is okay, if we have God as the Head of our life and are content with Him alone. It's dangerous when we act as if we don't need anyone, then we allow ourselves to become bitter and angry. There is nothing wrong with desiring the opposite sex; but if you are single, you have to learn to give that desire to God and become content with Him. Our self worth is not measured by having a man in our life; this is foolishness. We degrade ourselves, when we allow men, who don't even have all of their stuff together, to make us feel inadequate. It's time we start asking ourselves, "Why do I keep putting up with men who add nothing to my life?" We cannot keep blaming them for our issues; we have to allow God to show us who we really are. As my Pastor Raymond Horry says "Our God is an if/then God; if you do your part, He is faithful to do His part."

When I was forced to really take a good look at myself, I took a deep breath and spoke aloud every negative thing about me. The truth will set you free! When we really want help, we have to cry out; and we have to be truthful about our issues and pain. I urge you to do this same thing, speak out loud or write down every bad habit and/or struggle you have. It was after this examination of me that I learned to trust God to help me put my life in order.

I had just re-dedicated my life back to God. I had two small boys, ages one and three. Prior to me re-dedicating my life back to God, my children's father proposed. We were in the midst of planning a wedding, even though, I knew we were not ready for this life changing step. My flesh was saying, "Finally! I am your children's mother. We have been together over three years. You owe me this!" But, my spirit was saying, "You two are not ready. You don't have a church. Who is going to marry you? The relationship is too immature." There was definitely a battle between my flesh and my spirit! But, this is when, by the grace of God and a desire to do the right thing, I had to turn the volume down on my flesh and really listen to my Spirit.

The voice of our spirit is the still quiet voice we hear on the inside. In order to obey your spirit, you have to be really true to yourself and the situation. God will never make us do anything; life is choice driven. I had to be real with myself and ask, "Do I want to make this decision to get married knowing at this point we are not ready?" I am not talking about being ready financially and materially but ready spiritually. I kept asking myself, "Do I go ahead and do this, because it looks good to other people to see me married to my children's father, even though deep down I know we are not ready?"

Ladies, we have to stop thinking that because we have children with someone, this automatically qualifies them to be our husband, as this would make the situation better. If it were all good, we would have been married before having children. It is not the Will of God for us to have children out of wedlock, but it happens. Thank God we can repent, move on and still seek out the Will of God for our lives, including whether or not the father of our children is the one we should marry. We, automatically, think it has to be God's Will for us to marry our child's father, but this is not always what's best for you or the child. Seek God; ask Him

His Will.

In the midst of planning a wedding, I went to church and gave my life back to God. Now, you cannot shack up (live with someone who is not your husband), go to church, get saved (or re-dedicate your life back to God) and then, resume the same lifestyle. This is a curse and will always be a curse, until you change the situation. This is one of the biggest reasons why Believing women are being defeated and not walking in victory.

When we come into a relationship with God, the first thing we must do is get out of the sinful act of living with that man who is not our husband. God does not want to hear how many years you have invested in the relationship; so, do not tell him. Before coming to God; the father of my children and I had been living together for three years, but that had to change. I learned to truly trust God during this time; and to trust God, is to gain victory over that for which we trust Him. The more we obey the Voice of God, our inner man, the easier it is to overcome the flesh. I can see, now, how God was positioning me for a blessing. I feel certain if I had fought God in this process and continued to shack up, then, instead of being positioned for a blessing, I would have positioned myself to be under a curse. When God is trying to remove what's hindering us, He's just displaying His Love for us.

I knew, in my heart, the church I had joined was where God wanted me to be. Even though my children's father and I were no longer living together, we were still engaged to be married and trying to figure out on our own the Will of God. I inquired about the church's pre-marital classes and learned it was not the usual premarital class but a pre-engagement class. The requirements for the class were:

1. You have to be a child a God
2. You cannot be engaged
3. You cannot have a ring
4. You cannot be planning or have a date set to be married

We qualified on the first requirement but were disqualified on two through four. In order to receive counseling for marriage from this particular pastor, we had to call off the engagement. Remember, we were not exactly ready for marriage in the first place, so why not give up something for which we were not prepared. To the flesh, this makes no sense; but to the spirit, it makes all the sense in the world. The spirit knows what is now and what's to come; our flesh only knows what we can see.

Now, it was test time. Not only did I give back the ring and discontinued all wedding plans, we stopped having sex. I know you are probably thinking "What?" This was the best decision I could have ever made. Pre-marital classes are popular in today's culture, but what's really needed is counseling before even considering an engagement. In my opinion, there should be no wedding plans and no rings involved during the counseling. This is not biblical but wise. When couples are in premarital classes, their flesh is so involved in the planning process; they are really trying not to hear anything against what they already plan to do. Planning a wedding at the same time you are in counseling only makes it harder to do the right thing, because every time God shows you something, you are thinking about your dress, ring, guest list, etc. God has me sharing this, so I know someone needs to hear it. Do not get caught up in this type of situation for the sake of being married. The wedding lasts only a few hours, but marriage is for life. God hates divorce, especially if it could have been avoided. Seek God before marrying; you will be glad you did. My husband and I find satisfaction in knowing we prepared for marriage the right way; and on those days when we ask, "Why did I get married?" God comforts us and reassures us He is in it every step of the way.

Having babies out of wedlock is why many of us are frustrated, angry and bitter; it is time to gain victory in this area. We are having kids with men who have no intention of marrying us, and it is time we take responsibility for our bad decisions. We have to stop blaming the men because, unless we were raped, we made a conscious decision to lie down in the bed. We Believing women should know better. We are disconnecting from God for a night of pleasure, and when the relationship does not go as planned, we become angry and bitter. My purpose is not to make anyone feel bad, but this is what God spoke to my heart, because I was one of these women. I knew Christ before meeting the father of my children. I was in church but got back in the world, when I met him. I was not as mature as I am now, but I was a Believer.

During the entire time we dated, God was tugging at my heart. It, literally, took me five years to respond to God calling me back; but keep in mind, He doesn't promise you five years or even five days. The day we hear God's voice calling us back, scripture tells us,

*Today if you hear his voice, do not harden your hearts.* Hebrews 3:7-8

When I finally got back to church, I had two small children. I was ready to change, but my children's father was not. God spoke to my heart, "He is not your husband, and therefore, he does not owe you anything; his obligation is to your children." Once I got that revelation, the decision was much easier to make. I am not taking responsibility away from fathers, but I am saying, "Focus on you." Once I began to focus on my own mistakes, it made me think how God felt, when I stepped out of His Will and ended up pregnant out of wedlock. This brought me to a place of repentance, where I was able to see my own faults and sins and not just those of my children's father. I, first, had to apologize to God and acknowledge that I messed up.

So many Believing women are in this situation; it was me, too, until I turned it over to the Lord and gained the victory. My children's father did, eventually, hop on board; but I had to focus on my relationship with God and my children and continue to pray for him that God's Will, not my own, would be done. My flesh still wanted their daddy, but I was, finally, learning to follow the spirit that leads to life versus the flesh that leads to death. Sex before marriage does not please God. In God's eyes, it does not matter how long you've been with the man; the world honors common law marriage, not God.

I am so grateful and humbled to share my story and give God all the glory. The decision was not easy, but the more I put my trust in God, the more He graced me to go through. Dropping the engagement and beginning pre-engagement classes with Pastor was the best thing we could have done. We could have been married at the court house or by another pastor and still attended my church; but we both, for once, ignored our flesh and yielded to the spirit. Our situation is not perfect; but because we took the time to seek His approval, we can be guaranteed everything will work out for our good, as long as we keep God in it.

What is your struggle? Whatever it is, give it over to God. I promise you He will not fail you. He will keep you; and as you learn to trust in Him, your life will never be the same. You can control your flesh; with God, all things are possible!

## Why Renew the Mind?

We are dying spiritually, because we believe the lies of the enemy. He fills our heads with lies, telling us we're failures: "That's just the way you are. You can never change. You will never be healed. You will never find love; you are ugly; you are fat; you are a bad person." He will try to place all of these lies in your mind. But he is a liar, the master of lies; and there's no truth in him.

Satan knows the only way to get to the heart of God is to mess with His children. It's really not even about us; he understands the love God has for his children. Every soul Satan wins, he takes right to God and brags about it. It breaks the heart of God to see His daughters defeated because we believe all of these lies about ourselves. God sent His Only Begotten Son so that we may live and have life and have it in abundance, yet we are being defeated. Every time we believe the lies of the enemy, we give him the glory. His main objective is to not lose a single soul to God; thus, whenever he recognizes we are searching or coming to know truth, he begins to bombard our minds with lies.

We must renew our minds after we accept Jesus as our Lord and Savior.

*But be transformed by the renewing of your mind.* Romans 12:2

We can no longer think the way we did, when we were in the world; we have to transform into a new person by renewing the mind. We can no longer think it is okay to live with someone who is not our husband, or hangout in bars/clubs, or gamble on the boat. You have to tell yourself, "I am a new creature; old things have passed away, and I no longer desire these things." Our biggest spiritual high is during the first one to three months after receiving Christ (some don't go that long). We expect for everything in life to be smooth sailing; but once we say, "Yes" to Jesus, it is Satan's daily job to fight against the renewal of our mind. He will come at you with all sorts of things; that's when you have to tell him, "The old me has passed away, I am a new creature."

The day of Salvation our spirits were born again, not our minds. Satan knows sin first takes place in our mind. It starts with a thought, and if we toy around with the thought too long, eventually, we will act on it.

*We take captive every thought to make it obedient to Christ.* 2 Corinthians 10:5

Do whatever you have to do; I laugh at the enemy when he brings something foolish to my mind. You might have to sing or hum a praise and worship song, or just repeat the name Jesus, whatever works for you. I guarantee the enemy will flee. We have to fight for our Salvation everyday!

The enemy will tell you Christianity is too hard or too boring or just not worth it; if you are not feeding yourself the Word of God, you will believe everything he says. He is a liar and a deceiver and there's no truth in him. We must transform into a new person by renewing our mind. I know it sounds hard, but I tell you, from experience, it is possible to overcome. The more you say, "No," to your flesh, the more God will grace you; it will be become easier and easier. Also, every time we say, "Yes," to the flesh, the harder our walk will be, because we are giving power to the flesh. I can testify, by God's grace, I have gained the victory over cigarettes, marijuana, alcohol, sex before marriage, gambling and the battle of my mind. Praise God!

I have struggled most of this journey with letting the enemy condemn me with thoughts of, "I am not good enough." "I am not perfect enough." "God cannot really use me until I get certain things right." It is true, we have to begin working on the sin and mess of our lives; but we have to know God called us anyway. We do not have to feel bad about our struggles of the flesh. Instead, take them to God; it is only with Him we are able to overcome. As long as we are willing to change, He is with us to help. Some behaviors might be more difficult to conquer than others, but taking it one day at a time with God and a renewed mind, nothing is impossible. No longer worry and live in fear. We have to purpose to keep our minds on the right things.

*Whatever is true, whatever is worthy of reverence and honorable and seemly whatever is just, whatever is pure, whatever is lovely and lovable, whatever is kind and winsome and gracious, if there is any virtue and excellence, if there is anything worthy of praise, think on and weigh and take account of these things [fix your mind on them].* Philippians 4:8

Do these things and your mind will be at rest, and you will gain the peace of God that surpasses all understanding. Focusing on Jesus will guard your mind. Only when our minds are at rest can we think clearly and make wise decisions. A busy mind, always wandering and worrying, can miss what the Holy Spirit is saying; there is no need to be anxious about anything. One of the biggest tricks of the enemy is distraction. If we are busy trying to figure things out on our own, we will miss God every time. Some days are better than others, but we can't go too far in our minds before saying, "My God can handle this. It's a fact, I can't handle it; but on the day of Salvation, He told me that He will never leave me nor forsake me, so whatever I am going through, I rest in knowing He is with me." When you are living for God, there is purpose in everything. We must stay mindful that God is teaching us in our waiting state. Renew your mind and learn to trust Him.

## Having the Right Attitude

Once we gain victory over our mind, it is much easier to display the right attitude. Whatever we are feeling in our heart will definitely show in our attitude. Remember, God is all about winning souls. Too many Believers get saved and then portray a selfish attitude (I got mine so you better get yours). This is far from being Godly. By the grace of God, you are saved; it has nothing to do with what you have done or how good you are.

*For it is by grace you have been saved, through faith - and this not from yourselves, it is the gift of God - not by works, so that no one can boast.* Ephesians 2:8-9

If not for God's mercy, you would not be saved. You should show that same merciful attitude toward others that God shows to you. God is doing a new thing in the earth realm, and every Christian should be trying to win as many souls as possible, thus having the mind and attitude of Christ. Your attitude says and means a lot. After you are saved, people watch you; intentionally or unintentionally, they are watching. The world wants to know if this Christianity thing is real; they are waiting to see if you mess up.

God tells us to "...*walk in the Spirit*" Galatians 5:16

by practicing, doing, engaging in

*...the fruit of the Spirit: love, joy, peace, long suffering, gentleness, goodness, faith, meekness, temperance: against such there is no law.*
Galatians 5:22

This means to have the right attitude. I don't think, as Christians, we emphasize this as much as we should. God calls every Christian to put on daily the fruit of the spirit. When you have a humble and grateful attitude, it is easy to love and be patient, because you are mindful of what God gives to you. Early in my walk with the Lord, I remember Him saying, "You're Salvation is not about you but about those around you." At that moment, I received this; and it still pushes me to keep going. I tell myself, "If I mess up, then I may cause someone else (my husband, children, sisters, cousins, co workers) to mess up, and I don't want to be accountable for that."

I know Christians who have the worst attitudes. It all comes down to selfishness, not realizing their Salvation is not about them. God did not save you because you were one of his favorites; He loves everybody and shows no favoritism, but He does show mercy to whom he wants. He has shown me so much mercy; how dare I not give it back. It is easy for me to be patient, because my God has been more than patient with me. I can be long suffering, because He waited for me long after He called me. Our God has not called us to do anything He has not done before us. We should love others, because He is the epitome of love, and He showed the ultimate love by the giving of His Son.

As women, we often feel we have a right to display a bad attitude, because we want to show our anger and hurt. We want the world to know we are scorned, because we have been cheated on, because we can't get any help from the dead beat dads, or because of our poor upbringing. Whatever your issue, once you become a child of God, express your deepest hurt and pain to Him but know that your situation does not justify your behavior. All things are new when you come to know Christ. Whatever you went through is for someone else, for your testimony giving God the glory for the victory. A bad attitude only hurts you, robbing you of your joy and energy that can be used to praise God. Regardless of our issues, we are still standing, we are not defeated; thus, everything we do should be done unto the Lord, not people. Turn your attitude around and be thankful God has still kept you through it all. God is worthy of having our all, including our attitude. Let Him do a new thing in you by transforming your attitude; it is the least you can do for Him.

## My Body is the Temple

*"Don't you know that you yourselves are God's temple and that God's Spirit lives in you? If anyone destroys the temple, God will destroy him; for God's temple is sacred, and you are that temple."*
1Corinthians 3:16-17

I love to quote this scripture to those who like to say, "The Bible doesn't say that you cannot smoke or drink." God does not use those exact words, but He tells us our bodies are our temples, so how can we conclude inhaling smoke into our temples where the Spirit of God dwells is okay? God does not crave cigarettes; your spirit is not addicted, your flesh is. I smoked cigarettes prior to becoming a Believer; but after accepting Christ as my Savior, I remember the feeling I had in my spirit.

I am so conscious of God being alive as a spirit on the inside of me. As Believers, when we commit sins within our bodies, such as fornication, drinking and smoking, we hate to think about Jesus dwelling on the inside of us; but not thinking about it or ignoring it does not change the fact that it's true. We have to keep a God-conscious mind. Things your body (flesh) wants to do, I guarantee your spirit does not; places where your body (flesh) wants to go, I guarantee your spirit does not. The Spirit is Holy; the Spirit is God living on the inside of you. Start treating the Holy Spirit as the real, true, living person He is. Ask Him before committing any sin, "Do you want to lay with this person who's not my husband; do you want to get high?" I promise you the answer will be, "No," every time. Have you ever tried to hide sin from someone? For whatever reason, you did not want to be caught, so you hid, ducked and dodged in order not to be caught in the act. Even in your ducking and dodging, God is right there inside you. You can never hide from him.

You might not struggle the addictions of drugs, alcohol or sex, but are you taking care of your physical body by exercising, eating right and drinking plenty of water? Take care of your temple. If you are not fit and healthy, the enemy knows you are no good to the Kingdom; and he is trying to trick our generation with a spirit of laziness and overeating. He knows if you are always tired or overweight, you cannot be used to the fullest; and eventually, your health will become a hindrance. When the Holy Spirit calls, your body is too tired and sluggish to wake up to pray in the morning. Being overweight opens the door to low self-esteem and insecurity. How can we glorify God, when we don't feel secure about ourselves? It's not about being a particular size; it's about being healthy and fit.

You may ask what this has to do with a relationship with God; it has everything to do with it. If we want to fully live in our God given purpose, we have to deepen our relationship in order for Him to speak to us about our purpose. Then, we have to receive it by faith and spend the rest of our days working to achieve it. There will be some easy days, some hard days, but this is why we have to purpose to give no room to the enemy. You have a purpose, but so does the enemy; his purpose is to stop yours, and he will use everything he can, including your health and body.

## Victory Prayer

Heavenly Father, I thank you, in the name of Jesus that I have been delivered from my flesh. I thank you that I am new creature and old things have passed away. I purpose in my heart to obey my spirit man from this moment forward. I ask you to strengthen me right now, so I will not continue to be weak and defeated. Teach me to walk in the authority you gave me. I thank you that I have a renewed mind, so I may begin to change the way I think about my circumstances and situations. I thank you that I no longer have a bad attitude about my past and failures. I will handle adversities with a right attitude. I thank you that I have been renewed, even in my physical body. My body is the temple in which you dwell, and I will never offend you by abusing or bringing harm to it. I thank you for your mercy and forgiveness of past offenses. Thank you for being such a loving God and a God of second chances. In Jesus name, I pray, Amen.

From Defeat To Victory

## Chapter 2 - Victory over Your Spiritual Walk

As we purpose to gain victory over our flesh, we are, in return, gaining victory over our spirits. It's the Will of God for every person, who confesses Jesus as Lord and Savior, to gain victory over their spiritual walk and not be defeated by the enemy. We are more than conquerors (Romans 8:37), and greater is He that is in us than he that is in this world. Jesus Christ came so that we may have life and have it in abundance. I want to know how I can have this abundant life! God deals with us in different ways, according to our unique personalities and the purpose and plan he has for us individually. We have to work out our Salvation daily; it's not always easy, but it's possible and the rewards are more than worth it.

If God wanted, He could make us obey Him or destroy us right on the spot. Because of his faithfulness and His love for us, He gave us free will to do whatever we choose to do. Can you imagine how it satisfies God when we freely choose to love Him, live righteously and serve Him? I am complimented when someone tells me they cannot wait to get to where I am spiritually; I always let them know they can have the same, or even better, relationship with God. It is up to you how deeply your relationship grows; it's not that God is using me because I am special, but because He can trust me to obey Him.

I spend lots of time nourishing my relationship with God through prayer, studying His Word and purposing to live righteously. I am a living witness it is possible to be "souled out" to the Gospel. I see so many Believing women compromise their relationship with God for the sake of trying to fit in/be accepted. No one wants be looked at as "holier than thou;" but when we keep God our main priority, it does not matter what anyone says or thinks. We cannot allow worldly distraction to keep us from growing in our relationship with God. I am no more special or deserving than another person. The difference is that I choose not to compromise my walk with God by hanging out with people who will cause me to separate from Him.

Are you at a place in your life where you know God is calling you to go higher in Him? You've joined a church, serve in a Ministry and somehow still feel as if you are not growing? If this is where you are, you have to take time to evaluate the situation and yourself. You have to start asking God and yourself questions: Are you at the right church? Are you doing things that are hindering your walk? Do you really believe in the Word of God for yourself? You have to ask questions and watch for signs that follow those questions. Then, as God reveals to you what is hindering your walk with Him, do something about it.

The very first time I accepted Christ into my life I was around twenty. Even though as a little girl, my grandmother took me to church; after the age of ten, I can't recall being in church. One day a friend invited me to a choir concert at her church, and that night I received Christ. I remember being so excited; my spirit felt alive for the first time in my adult life. Because my spirit was hungering for God, I decided to attend a Sunday Service with my friend, despite my earlier encounter with her Pastor. This Pastor, whose name I will not mention, claimed to be a prophet. We went to her house, so she could prophesy to me. Remember, this was new to me, so I did not see the situation the way I do now; but I did find it strange that as she was prophesying, there was an ashtray full of cigarette butts next to her,.

I ignored what my common sense was telling me about this smoking pastor and decided to attend the worship service. I recall my spirit searching and hungering for something but not being fed. I continued attending these services for a month, and then, went right back to my worldly life. When you don't know what your spirit is hungering for and how to feed it, the world, with all of its sinful ways, is where you return. I believe part is our responsibility and part is the responsibility of the spiritual leader under whom you are sitting. It is crucial you find a spiritual leader who is living a holy lifestyle. Pray about it, because God will reveal, and He will direct. God allowed me to experience this, so I could tell others and encourage you by revealing I did throw in the towel and did not assume all pastors were living foul.

God tells us in Jeremiah 3:15,

*Then I will give you Shepherds after my own heart, who will lead you with knowledge and understanding.*

Many people have decided not to attend or join a church because of the behavior of a pastor. It is hurtful when you realize the pastor, you have held in high esteem, has not been living a righteous life; but know God will never hurt you, so do not let an unrighteous pastor keep you from hearing from God. You must confess, "Lord I am hurt by this person, but I know You have nothing to do with it; and even though, I cannot trust man right now, I thank You that You can always be trusted. And, Lord, give me discernment, so I will know when any person is operating in any spirit that is not of You."

As Christians we have to take responsibility for our part. When we are praying, studying God's Word and purposing to grow our relationship with God (not the Pastor), this reduces the chances of being deceived by anyone.

The Word of God says,

*My sheep know my voice, and they follow me.* John 10:27

So, when I hear about pastors doing ungodly things and leading thousands of people, I think shame on that pastor but double shame on the people for allowing it. We are responsible for nurturing our spiritual maturity, so we will know what is God and what is not

God. Unfortunately it's true, not all pastors are living holy and righteous lives, but don't let these few keep you from finding the pastor God has sent for you.

He tells us in Jeremiah 3:15,

*I will give you Pastors according to my own heart, who shall feed you knowledge and understanding.*

If you don't believe that, then you don't believe God's Word is true.

## Why a Church Home?

Once God sends you a pastor, you have found your church home. Many debate the importance of going to church; but He tells us, thus He will send us Pastors, and that Pastor will be connected to a church. You can be a Christian, accept God into your heart and never attend church. We can come up with many reasons not to attend church, but Believers who are hungry for God and His Kingdom understand we do not attend church because we have to but because we want to. God gives us the many benefits in His Word for becoming a part of a church: to edify one another, to obtain spiritual gifts, to build up, to use our gifts and talents, to pray for one another. Shouldn't the church be the first place you use your gifts and talents?

Sometimes when I am not sure what to do, I use the famous saying, "What would Jesus do?" (WWJD). I believe Jesus would go to church, He would not make excuses or justify why He could not go. Many do not have the choice: they are in hospitals, confined to their beds, etc., God understands; He will definitely supply their needs. For those of us who just give excuses because we don't feel like going, I suggest you switch places with someone who wants to go but can't. Having a church home is critical after receiving Jesus Christ into your life. You can be saved at a funeral, the mall, a grocery store, someone's house or in church.

Wherever, afterwards you must ask God to lead you to the right church. Do not just assume He wants you at the church where you were saved, maybe He does, maybe not; let Him direct you.

We should not make this huge decision based on the location of the church, the length of the service, the music the choir sings, the church your family has always attended. There are plenty of good Bible teaching churches, but God has one specifically for you and for this season of your life. Sometimes there might be reasons to find a church with shorter services due to your work schedule or because you do not have a car, but don't look for a church with an hour service, so you can be out quickly to spend your Sunday fulfilling your desires. That is having a wrong motive and being led by your flesh not your spirit. God knows your situation and He understands; He will lead you somewhere based on your circumstance. God knows your heart; He knows whether your motives and intentions are right; we can never fool Him. Ask Him before joining any church, "God, is this the place for me?" It has nothing to do with whether it's a good church or bad church. God knows exactly what we need, what kind of teaching we will receive and what ministry gifts we will bring to the church.

When God leads you to join a church, He is the only one who can tell you to leave. It's not your decision. People leave a church for the most foolish reasons: the pastor said something you didn't agree with, you were not recognized for something you did, or you were not chosen to be a leader. Whatever the reason, if God placed you there, He is the only one to release you. This eliminates "church hopping," and also part of God maturing us, because there will be times when you will be uncomfortable and offended. This is when we pray to see God in the situation and learn what He's trying to teach us. You cannot decide to leave a church based on emotions. We must be led by God; we have to acknowledge God in all of our ways. When we make decisions without Him, we are opening the door to the enemy; and the enemy loves confusion and mess. Ultimately, the devil wants you to leave the church completely; but when God places you somewhere, you know you are there with a purpose and it gives you something on which to stand. God will place us under the right pastor, and we are to follow the pastor He placed over us as he follows God.

When you are at the right church, your toes will and should get stepped on; you should feel uncomfortable, a lot of the time, during the Pastor's Message. Whatever sin you are struggling with will be the subject, time after time, until you conquer it. This is the love of God. It's His way of letting you know He knows all about it, and He is trying to clean you up. You should not sit in a church that does not speak against sin. God says He HATES sin and so should every Christian; we don't hate the person, we hate the sin. You should not be at a church in agreement with living with someone who is not your husband ("shacking up"), in agreement with homosexuality or that does not teach Holy living. I am not saying those who practice these things should not come or that the Pastor and congregation should not welcome them, but you have to let them know it is a sin and against the express Will of God.

I know, by the spirit of God, He is doing a new thing. The fact God is using me to write this book confirms it. A lot of things I speak about I have learned firsthand, and I have no regrets, because I told God I would use every mistake to help someone else and glorify Him in the process. Some things I have learned from talking to other Believers and nonbelievers, but most of it came from the Spirit of God through my spending time with Him. None of this would even be possible if God had not placed me under a pastor after his own heart. If we were able to obtain everything we needed on our own, there would be no need for teachers, doctors, pastors, leaders, evangelists, prophets, etc.; God would have just taught us all on His own. That is possible, but God has purpose for everything and everybody. I thank Him that I have grown from everything I am sharing with you; and through having a church home, I have matured as a Christian, woman, wife, mother, sister, friend, and employee.

Most of all, I have learned firsthand the importance of having a church home. If you're not sure about your church home, take time to pray and ask God about it. Do not look at the facts: it's your families' church, you've been there for years, you don't know of any other churches. Do not let these excuses keep you from the blessings God has for you in another church. Many stay at churches because they are comfortable and fearful of change; where God is taking this generation of Believers there's room for neither. Comfort and fear are guaranteed to block your blessings and will slowly kill your spirit and your relationship with God. Even if you feel uncomfortable now, know that it's God; receive Him, pray and let Him lead you to the right place.

On the other hand, if you do not have a church home, ask God to send you to the right place. You may have to visit around, or maybe, He will show you right away; but whatever you do, do not sit at home. That's what the enemy wants you to do; then, after so long, he will trick you into thinking you don't have to go to church. The Word tells us

*not giving up meeting together, as some are in the habit of doing, but encouraging one another—and all the more as you see the Day approaching.* Hebrews 10:25

While we are the church, individually; we also come together corporately to uplift, encourage and worship together. This is how we have church. Do not be fooled by the enemy; he is the only one who will tell you, you don't have to go to church.

## Serving in Ministry

Once God leads us to a church home, it is time to serve! Every Believer is called to be servant; Jesus Christ was the perfect example of servant. You might now be saying, "It does not take all that," but I am telling you, "Yes it does!" God is trying to teach this generation His best for our lives. I know, by faith, there are other women, like me, in this generation who want to live out the Perfect Will of God for our lives. God is gracing me to go through this spiritual journey, so I can encourage and help someone else. It is time we, Believers, stop living only part of the definition of a Christian. We do not pray the Prayer of Salvation, and that's the end of it; it's only the beginning.

After receiving Christ, it is time to go to work. It's time to make Christianity part of who we are, not just what we do. We do not win over unbelievers only by word of mouth but, also, with our lifestyle. When we were living in the world: going to clubs, happy hour, the boat, etc., it was what we did; it was normal for us. This is the same frame of mind you need when serving in ministry. The difference is that there is fulfillment when serving God; and when we do what we do unto the Lord, there is automatic peace, joy, healing and deliverance for you and your family. We serve no one but God. Once you find a church home, there is a guaranteed assignment there for you; you are greatly needed! When I first joined my church, I was told to pray about the Ministry I should join. You might already have an idea of how you want to serve if you like to sing, cook or work with children; but even with these talents, you have to be prayerful about what God's Will is for you to do in the church. I did not have a clue; but as I took this to God, in prayer, He placed on my heart to join the Spiritual Counseling Ministry. The name itself was enough to cause fear in a babe in Christ. I remember asking, "God, are you serious?"

After discovering a Spiritual Counselor's responsibility (to pray for and meet the spiritual needs of those who respond to the Pastor's Invitations of Salvation, Accepting the Holy Spirit or Re-dedication to Christ), I told God I couldn't do what He was calling me to do. In spite of all my fears, I obeyed the voice of God. Now, when I think about it, I wonder how many Believers ignore what God is calling them to do because of fear or feeling incompetent. How many Believers are walking around today in disobedience? How many people have had their blessings delayed because they didn't obey God by saying or doing what He told them to do? I'm sure I've missed the mark many times and will miss it again, because I am human; but I will never purpose to be disobedient, especially after experiencing the fulfillment of being used by a Mighty Powerful All Knowing God.

By serving in church ministry, Christians show their gratitude to a graceful, merciful God. Serving says, "Lord, I thank You, I owe You me; serving is the least I can do." Coming from a woman who has spent more than enough time in the world doing my own thing (going to every club, on every boat, in every bar or tavern), I confess to you, right now, there is no greater joy than serving in the house of the Lord. No paycheck could add up to it. It does not matter what Ministry you are a part of; one Ministry is no more important than another. If you are already serving in ministry, pray and ask God to renew your passion for it; rededicate yourself, and remember you are serving a God who is worthy and deserving.

## The Importance of Praise and Worship

Praise and worship, along with the Word of God, is the survival kit for every Christian. In chapter one, I compared first becoming a Christian to being on "cloud nine" anywhere from 1 day to 6 months. Why do we experience this huge spiritual high and a few months, or even a day, later live as if we aren't saved at all. I've experienced this firsthand; I went back to the world twice after receiving Christ. So many of us receive Christ in our hearts but don't have a clue how to keep from going back to the world. One thing I do know, if you are hungry for God, are truly tired of sin in your life and desire to live right, (regardless of where you are and how you are living right now) just say, "Lord I need you to help me, I want to change but I don't know how,." with a sincere heart and praise Him for the Victory, I guarantee the enemy will flee; and God will release the grace needed for you to overcome.

I wish I could say since becoming a Christian, life has been easy, but this is far from the truth. Unfortunately, I can't tell you I wake up every Sunday excited to go to the house of the Lord. Before receiving Christ, we were friends with the enemy who loves us when we are lonely, depressed, have no vision nor dreams, no hope for tomorrow; but when we become children of God, we have a renewed hope, we no longer have to fight our own battles and the enemy can't stand it. So, now it's his job to talk us out of our Salvation. He reminds us of our past and the things God has already forgiven. His plan is to keep us in bondage with our past. This is why, I believe, most baby Christians can barely last 3 months before going back into the world.

Praise and worship is our weapon; it's our key to survival. Along with studying God's Word, we have to start our day with praise and thanksgiving. I know you've heard it before, "There are two times to praise God: when you feel like it and when you don't." Even when you don't know what to pray, start by praising God for who He is and for all He has done. Praise opens the ears of God. We don't get His attention because we have cried long and hard or whined. God is not moved by our circumstances and situations:

*For my thoughts are not your thoughts, neither are your ways my way.* Isaiah 59:8

Praise your way out of every situation; praise Him for turning your situation around while you are still going through it. Thank Him for being Alpha and Omega (the beginning and the end); thank Him for your salvation; thank Him for providing and making a way out of no way. This is how to acknowledge God and make the devil out to be the liar he is. One of the enemy's biggest tricks is to keep us distracted with what we see and how we feel. We must walk by faith and not by sight. What you see with the natural eye is temporary and subject to change. We have to stay in the spirit and see things the way God does. Instead of complaining, praise Him, especially for the small blessings; this is how we prepare for bigger blessings. We all want more and bigger stuff; but if you want God to bless you with more, you have to appreciate and take care of what you already have. This eliminates an unappreciative, discontented spirit which is another way the enemy will push you right back into the world.

We feel we should have more stuff and become impatient with God when we don't get what we want when we want it. Eventually we figure out how to get it on our own, not realizing we are disconnecting ourselves from God and His protection and His provision. When we are content and learn to praise God anyhow, in the midst of our praise, He will reveal to us exactly why He is not giving us that for which we think we are ready. He tells us in his Word,

*Do not be anxious about anything but in everything, by prayer and petition, with thanksgiving; present your request to God. And the peace of God, which transcends all understanding, will guard your hearts and your minds in Christ Jesus.* Philippians 4:6-7

Praise brings contentment and, as Believers, we are called to be content in every situation. Praise, along with worship, is powerful and makes the devil flee. Praise God and worship Him with your whole heart, mind, body and soul. Worship is an expression of our love for God. Although we worship in song, we also worship with our hearts by loving Him and placing no one above Him, with our minds by staying focused on Him and His many promises, and with our bodies by saying no to premarital sex and not abusing our temple with drugs and alcohol. We are acknowledging our bodies as the temple in which the Holy Spirit dwells. We worship with our soul by saying, "Yes" to God's Will. We acknowledge Him in all our ways, so He will make our paths straight. I pray that you meditate on this chapter, not because it is more important but because praise and worship intimidates the enemy. There is no way he can hang around praise and worship.

## Store His Word in Your Heart

Therefore you shall lay up these My Words in your [minds and] hearts and in your [entire] being, and bind them for a sign upon your hands and as forehead bands between your eyes. And shall teach them to your children, speaking of them when you sit in your house and when you walk along the road, when you lie down and when you rise up. And you shall write them upon your door post of your house and on your gates. That your days be multiplied in the land which your Lord swore to your fathers to give them, as long as the heavens are above the earth. Deuteronomy 11:18-21

The Word is not only for us alone but also for our children. God promises our days will be multiplied when we store His Word in our hearts. I don't want to sound insensitive or cruel, but sometimes I wonder what things could have been prevented if only we had God's Word stored in our hearts. I understand things happen to both Believers and nonbelievers, but I am almost positive many of us have lost loved ones who possibly could be alive today if only someone had the Word in his heart. Not only had they known the Word but had been the Word. It's not enough to know the Word; you have to be the Word illustrated by righteous living and true worship. You must have a lifestyle to match the Word.

*So get rid of all uncleanness and the rampant outgrowth of wickedness, and in humble (gentle, modest) spirit receive and welcome the Word which implanted and rooted [in your hearts] contains the power to save your souls. But be doers of the Word [obey the message], and not merely listeners to it.* James 1:21-22

The Word of God brings healing, deliverance, restoration, hope, peace, joy, freedom and truth. The enemy himself knows the power of the Word of God, thus he likes to keep it from God's children. As you begin to read and study the Bible, the enemy will tell you it's boring, you can't understand it, it makes you sleepy. Each of these excuses makes sense to your flesh; but the Word of God is not flesh, it is spirit. You have to be in the spirit when you read it.

*For the word of God is quick, and powerful, and sharper than any two edged sword, piercing even to the dividing asunder of soul and spirit, and of the joints and marrow, and is a discerned of the thoughts and intents of the heart.* Hebrews 4:12

You cannot take God's Word as a joke or make a mockery out of it; God knows the motive and heart of each of us, whether you realize it or not. You have to pray before you open your Bible; ask God to cleanse your heart and get rid of any and everything not like him. You have to prepare your mind forgetting, to the best of your ability, worldly cares and get ready to receive from God as you read His Word.

I learned to understand the Word of God as I grew hungry for God. When you get to a point where you can't wait to get home just to get into God's Word, then you are where God wants you to be. We have to become a thirsty generation of women. Whenever the

Holy Spirit prompts you to read your Bible, you must be obedient. I recommend you start anywhere. The Bible, as a whole, is vitally important. Although the New Testament may seem easier to grasp, it is necessary to understand the Old Testament, also, as it will help you understand God's promises and His faithfulness. Remember, one of the roles of the Holy Spirit is Teacher; ask him to help you and guide you into truth. He will do just that. When we study God's Word, we are feeding our spirit. We may not comprehend or remember everything right then; but when done with a clean heart and a right mindset, you are storing His Word in your heart. Then, when you go through trials, situations and tests, the Holy Spirit will bring God's Word back to your remembrance resulting in peace, joy, healing and deliverance for you from what God spoke to you in His Word. When you are in the midst of your circumstance, it's too late then, to try to store up Word in your heart; you must be prepared.

You can find everything you need in God's Word. I challenge you to study and meditate upon it. You will find it is medicine to your soul. Whatever your symptom (problem), find out what the Word has to say about it; I guarantee there is an eternal cure for every problem, every situation you are going through.

*It is the truth that sets you free and whom the Son has set free is free indeed.* John 8:32, 36

## Victory Prayer

Lord, I worship You in spirit and in truth! I thank You right now for strength to walk this spiritual journey. I thank You for directing me to the church where You will have me to be, a church that is led by a Pastor according to Your own heart. I will not let friends and family clog my mind, my ears and drown out what You are speaking to me. I will obey my spirit man down to the letter. However you want me serve in the church, Lord, I am willing. I purpose in my heart to study Your Word and hide it in my heart, so the enemy cannot steal my joy and peace; instead I will praise and worship You. Thank You, Lord, for spiritual maturity. In Jesus name, Amen

## Chapter 3 - Victory over Your Daily Walk

Christianity is a lifestyle! It is not something you do only on Sunday; you cannot put it on and take it off at your convenience. It is not something you do once, and that's it. Some people believe once you confess Jesus Christ as your Savior, then, you are a Christian. They feel you never have to work on your lifestyle; you can continue to sin, do whatever you want to and still make it to Heaven. As Christians, in order to grow and mature as Believing women, we have to work out our Salvation daily. A Christian is who you are everyday; we are imitators of Christ. We are not perfect, we fall short daily; but we are to bring God glory in all we do: a trip to the grocery store, in the mall, at work.

Wherever we are, it is our responsibility, as a Christian, to carry God's presence. This does not mean carrying a bible, quoting scripture or pointing out sin in other people's lives; it means bringing the love of God. There is a time for everything; and when you are God-conscious, the Holy Spirit will always prompt you how to handle people and situations. We all deal with the same day to day irritations: being stuck in traffic, waiting in long checkout lines, the worker at the drive thru with the bad attitude. All of these are to test us. How we handle people and deal with situations that inconvenience us, help us get to where God is taking us. That person with the bad attitude may need a smile or a kind word; the cashier working the long checkout line might need to see a Christian demonstrate patience. We are Ambassadors of Christ; we are to walk in the fruit of the Spirit daily.

*This I say then, Walk in the Spirit, and ye shall not fulfil the lust of the flesh.* Galatians 5:16

You have to learn to give God glory every day, even when your day is not going as planned. When you are stuck in traffic, instead of murmuring and complaining, give God some praise. He is not surprised you're stuck in traffic and are going to be late for work. Maybe, He is causing you to be late to avoid that accident you might have been in had you been on time. You must purpose, in your heart, to see God every day in everything. Stop talking to God like He is not aware of the inconveniences in life; instead say, "Lord, show me You in this situation." I guarantee He will every time.

## Repent Daily

Because we are all imperfect people, we are going to sin daily! We sin knowingly (and unknowingly) with our actions, words and thoughts. Thus, we must repent of our sins every day, especially when convicted in our spirit. Conviction comes from God; He is prompting us to repent. Without conviction, there can be no repentance. Thank God when conviction comes; God is showing love towards you. Conviction defeats many Christians. Instead of receiving conviction as God's love, we allow condemnation to come upon us. Condemnation is not from God but of the devil. Condemnation makes you feel bad and not worthy of God, it feeds you lies about yourself.

*Therefore, there is no condemnation for those who are in Jesus Christ...* Romans 8:1

God NEVER condemns His children or makes them feel bad, but He will convict and chastise. Every child of God should memorize this advice from Our Father,

*If we confess our sins, He is faithful and just to forgive us our sins and cleanse us from all unrighteous.* 1John 1:9

I love this scripture, not only does God forgive us after confession; He cleanses us from ALL unrighteousness. It is so important to ask for forgiveness; never let the enemy condemn you and make you feel like you messed up so terribly that God will not forgive you. God will forgive us from any and every thing, as long as we ask Him with a sincere heart.

But, be careful not to abuse His willingness to forgive. You cannot have sex with someone who is not your husband (knowing that you are going to ask forgiveness and do it again) or continue to sin in any way because you know God will forgive you; this is not how it works. Sometimes, we really struggle with a situation, ask forgiveness with a sincere heart, and then, repeat the same sin. I would say to keep asking for forgiveness until you gain victory over that problem. God knows our hearts, we can never fool Him, He already knows and understands the things with which we struggle. Paul spoke of his struggling in the flesh, and I know most Christians have felt this way,

*For what I will to do, that I do not practice; but what I hate, that I do. If then, I do what I will not to do, I agree with the law, that it is good. But now, it is no longer I who do it, but sin that dwells in me. For I know that in me (that is, in my flesh) nothing good dwells; for to will is present with me, but how to perform what is good I do not find. For the good I will to do, I do not practice. Now if I do what I will not to do, it is no longer I who do it, but sin that dwells in me...who will deliver me from this body of death?* Romans 7:15-24

I thank God through Jesus Christ our Lord! If you have let this kind of behavior condemn you and hold you back in your Christian walk, know it is not you, but the sin that dwells within you. Only through Christ can you be delivered, thank Him for the victory!

## Obedience Brings Blessings

Obedience, obedience, obedience! This should be every

Christian's purpose in life. Obedience is exercising our faith muscles. It brings us closer to God and in return, grows and matures us in our Christian walk. My Pastor, Raymond D Horry, says it best, "Maturity is the evidence of the decreasing time it takes for you to obey the voice of God." Isn't parenting much easier when your children obey? You ask them to do something and quickly they reply, "Yes ma'am;" you ask them not to do something, and they reply "Okay." How wonderful this sounds to a mother, regardless of her child's age. Obedience makes life easier. It's sad I don't know any children this disciplined; but, as Christians, we are called to be this disciplined. Christianity is simply believing in Jesus Christ and obeying God's Word. The way we reward our children, when they are obedient to us, is the same way our Father likes to reward us, His children, when we obey His Word.

Obedience brings blessings; the more obedient we are, the more blessed we are. No obedience, no blessings. This does not mean you will never have things, because as long as you have money and the means, you can have anything you want, even without the presence of God. But blessings are far more than just things: good health for you and your children, a sane mind, a healthy marriage, prosperous children, walking in your calling, mobility of all your limbs, safety from harm and danger. All these blessings I will take over financial riches any day. You cannot equate being blessed to having money. For example, a nonbeliever can win the lottery or hit a big jack pot on the boat and call it a blessing. He may experience a temporary fulfillment of paying some bills here and there, buying some things he's wanted to buy; but sooner or later, he will experience sorrow because the presence of God is not present. Just because you call something a blessing does not mean it is. If you serve the devil, then, that's from whom your blessing comes.

We see, daily, how Hollywood stars blow money: indulging in drugs and illicit lifestyles; being unfaithful in their marriages; buying outrageously expensive homes. For most of them, there is no presence of the one true and living God. They are trying to fill voids with their blessings and still, are not happy. They are not led by God to spend their money; therefore, they lack fulfillment. You may be called a humanitarian, because you give to charities or feed the homeless; but if you have not acknowledged and accepted the Lord and Savior Jesus Christ, all of your giving is in vain.

We cannot work ourselves into Heaven by doing good works or deeds. Although, at any time, one can accept Jesus Christ, listen to His voice, be obedient and let Him lead in finances and giving. This is the way to receive God's blessings. This does not mean bad things will not happen,

*...he sendth rain falls on the just and on the unjust.* Matthew 5:45

but when God is in it, He will have our backs and work everything out for our good, because we have been obedient to Him. Obedience makes the difference between a Believer and a nonbeliever.

## Ask for Guidance and Direction

When you ask God to guide and direct you, He will place you on a path leading to the center of His will for your life. Asking Him for guidance is acknowledging Him as being in total control. God's guidance comes through His Word. Studying and meditating on His Word, brings truth and wisdom thus, helping us to make the right choices. Our God given freedom of choice can be a blessing or a curse. He has placed before us

*...that I have set before you life and death, blessings and curses. Now choose life,* Deuteronomy 30:19

*My child, listen to what I say, and treasure my commands...Then you will understand what is right, just, and fair, and you will find the right way to go.* Proverbs 2:1, 9

We should purpose everyday to be in the center of God's will for our lives. Understand, being in the center of God's will does not mean everything is peaches and cream. As we pray and study His Word, He will reveal His plans for our lives and begin to guide and direct us down the right path.

*For I know the plans I have for you, declares the Lord, plans to prosper you and not harm you, plans to give you hope and a future.* Jeremiah 29:11

You have to believe and trust, have faith in, God, the same way you trust that you are saved by faith, that He knows what is best for you.

*Trust God with all your heart and lean not to your own understanding; in all your ways acknowledge him, and he will make your paths straight.* Proverbs 3:5-6

As I began to ask God to lead and guide me, I have to admit it really wasn't easy, in my own strength; but with God, it became possible, as He graced me. I looked at my situation, all I had gotten myself into, and asked God, "What I have really got to lose in trusting you?" I saw I could do nothing in my own strength and was definitely tired of struggling and getting nowhere. Because I was determined to have a better life, I began to pray to God to order my steps, to lead me and to guide me; and He began to do just that. God is faithful and there for us when we turn to and trust in Him. As we pray for guidance and direction, He will begin to put our lives in order. He will, definitely, reveal to us things about ourselves with which we will have to change. When seeking to do God's will, we will have to get rid of some bad habits. We can no longer cheat on our taxes, ride around with bad car tags, improper license plates, warrants or write bad checks. We do these things when we are in the world; they cannot be a part of where God is taking us. We can never get ahead of God and think we have it all figured out. Thinking this way is the enemy trying to set us up for failure.

Every sin and every act of disobedience moves us off God's path; and the faster we recognize our sin(s) and repent, the sooner we can get back on the path and head to where we're going. We're going to make wrong turns; it's not the number of wrong turns we make but how quickly we get back to the right path. It's dangerous to toy around with being off the right path, because there is no protection off God's path. The enemy will come in like a flood as soon as we fall; he knows there is no covering, under God's umbrella of protection where we are safe and out of harm's way. The enemy cannot get under God's umbrella, but we can walk out from under it whenever we choose (whenever we allow ourselves to be in situations we know are sinful or with people who mean us harm). God is not obligated to keep us safe, when we go places we have no business going. If you do make it there and back, then praise God! Every day you sin and wake up the next day, you should thank God for His mercy and not practice that sin again. You made it out that time, but how do you really know if you will make it out again?

You have to know God as the All Knowing God He is. God is not surprised about things the same way we are. Why not ask an All Knowing God to direct you? Car accidents and plane crashes do not take God by surprise. If we only knew how many survivors there could have been, if someone had asked God to direct them. Asking gives Him permission to say, "Don't go right, turn left or vice verse; do not catch that flight; catch a later one." God speaks to us when we pray for direction. He is not obligated to keep us when we go places we should not go. I am mindful at all times that God shows mercy to whom he wants and when He wants. Never take advantage of the mercy of God. On the other hand, if He guides, He will provide. When you seek God and begin to ask Him to order your steps, He will take care of you. Let God order your steps every day.

*You guide me with your counsel leading me to a glorious destiny.*
Psalm 73:24

## Love Daily

Every Believer is called to love. God is love, and we are made in

His image and likeness. We draw unbelievers to Christ through love. It's time for Believers to stop looking down on the people of the world, as if God doesn't love them the same as He loves us. We are called to love those who are in the world; we do not love their sins, but we should love the person. Those in the world are doing exactly what a person without God does: killing, robbing, fighting, committing suicide, doing drugs, drinking, all of these things come with the territory of being in the world. You shouldn't expect anything else with the presence of God missing. We look at the world and judge them as if we are better.

As Believers, we are called to be the light in dark places, we are called to love. God is so serious about love He says,

*Love covers a multitude of sins.* 1 Peter 4:8

Are you so together that this will not benefit you? This love walk (daily living as a Christian not at church, not with your other Believing friends, but every day in the world) will allow you to gain victory over your daily life. Being a Believer is winning over people, drawing them to Christ, just by showing acts of kindness and love.

We were once of the world; we had bad attitudes and spoke disrespectfully, but God came and showed us love. We have to show that love to others. God is the epitome of love; you cannot genuinely have God and not have love in your heart. I understand some of us find it difficult to love, unconditionally, due to things that have happened in our lives. God knows and understands your difficulty displaying love, but there are no excuses. Some things you have to work on more than others; and when you are serious about God and the things of God, you will gain the victory. Your struggle will be your testimony; you will free someone else who finds it difficult to love.

Love is not an emotion; it is a choice and an action you have to purposely make. Loving someone is not always comfortable. Some people are easier to love than others; more than likely, these are the ones who need it the most. A decision to love is expressing God's love towards a person. Even when I did not love God, when he was nowhere on my mind, I was still on his heart. He still drew me to Him, through His Son, in the midst of my mess. In spite of everything: fornicating, drinking, cussing, clubbing, gambling and not doing His Will, He still loved me, He still called me. So, once I realized how much God loved me, I could not walk in love towards those who in the world or who didn't like me. We don't have to be best buddies, in order for me to love you. Even if you live a life of sin, I can still love you; I might not like the sin, but I can still love you.

*....Faith, hope and love and the greatest is love.* 1Corinthians 13:13

God tells us to walk in and be led by the Spirit; and as we walk in the Spirit, we will produce fruit. The first fruit is love followed by joy, peace, patience, meekness, temperance. (Galations 5:22) We must love; without love there is no Christianity. Christianity is based solely on love.

*For God so loved the world, that He gave His only begotten Son, that whosoever believes in Him shall not perish, but have eternal life.* John 3:16

What greater love is there other than this? God gave His Son for us while we were still sinners; how dare we not display that same love given to us to others. How will the world ever change if God cannot bring up a group of righteous Christians (followers of Christ), not righteous denominations (Catholic, Baptist, Jehovah Witness, Muslims, etc.)? All we are to do is follow Christ and His ways. I am not knocking any denomination; personally, I don't know much about them; all I know is that I follow Jesus. He is not a dead idol but a True and Living God.

We are to worship Him and Him alone; there is no other God in addition to Him. He is not prejudiced; He is not hateful and does not cause division. Either you are a Believer or a non-believer. It has nothing to do with the color of your skin, family background, or denomination. I guarantee Heaven will not be divided into sections. In Heaven, there will only be love, so if you cannot display love now, here on earth, or only show love to a particular group of people, why would you even want to go to Heaven? There is one blood flowing through all of mankind. There is only one Holy Spirit; either you have the Spirit of the True and Living God or the spirit of the devil. God is the only one who can heal, set free and deliver; and every Christian, who is filled with His Spirit, has the same power. There is really no debate about it, either you believe in His Word (the Holy Bible) or you don't. And if you believe, now it's time to gain some knowledge and believe in all of His Word, including Love.

## VICTORY PRAYER

Lord, I die to my flesh today, and I acknowledge You, not only inside the four walls of the church, but everywhere I go: to the grocery store, to the mall, to the beauty shop, to the nail shop. As I live, day to day, in this world, I will be mindful of You. I ask that You lead, guide, and direct my life as I deal with natural situations and circumstances. I confess I have allowed people and my past to control my attitude; this I release to You right now, and I ask that you create in me a clean heart. Help me to show compassion and to love even those I feel don't deserve it. I pray this in Jesus' name. Amen.

## Chapter 4 - Victory in Your Relationships

Every relationship should be enjoyed but also have purpose. Once we become Believers, it is important to begin evaluating all current relationships. Some of us became Believers while already in a relationship. In these situations, we must invite God in and ask Him to guide and lead us in order for His Will to be done. You might have to face the fact that the relationship is not meant to be. When we give our lives to God, we have to accept the fact that things change; but we can get stuck trying to prove to other people, and even ourselves, there is no change. We don't want to come off holier than thou, so we pretend to still like the same foolish things and conversations. We continue all of this with a feeling of conviction in the pit of our stomachs trying only to prove we are still the same person when, in reality, we are not; and we shouldn't be after receiving Jesus. The Word of God tells us in Romans 12:2,

*...not to conform to the world nor the things of the world. We have to understand that we are set apart from the world, and we have to act as such.*

We don't have to portray ourselves as better than others, but we have to show those who know us that we are changed. We cannot continue the same foolish conversations. We have to be able to, not only say that we have changed, but display it in our behavior and our speech. As we begin to live for and glorify God, we will be able to see the friendships worth keeping and those friendships that are toxic. We don't want to push away people who have a genuine respect for us and our walk with God, even if they are not saved. If they choose to hang around us, then there is a purpose in that. Perhaps they are curious about God and really want to know if this Christian thing really works before they try it. This can be either good or bad. We can be the light we are called to be to bring them into the Kingdom, or they can watch us fall right back into the things of the world; this is not the Will of God.

In the beginning of my walk, God spoke something to me that keeps me going. He said "Your salvation is not about you but about those around you." I found this to be true. By grace God saved us, and we have to be strong in the Lord so others will say, "Let me give this a try." Whatever they do after that is on them. Now, toxic relationships you want to get out of as soon as possible. In these relationships, you find yourself debating the Word and always trying to prove God is real. Do not tolerate these foolish relationships because we should never argue about the Word of God.

As women, most of us desire a relationship with a male as our mate and other females as friends (sisters). God understands. He created us to be the way we are, but we have to always examine our motives and the reasons we have certain people in our lives. Most of us feel we must have a group of friends; if we don't, then, we don't feel important or popular. We don't want to get caught up in relationships that feed our insecurities. Almost every toxic relationship is birthed out of loneliness and low self esteem; but when we say, "Yes," to Jesus, we must learn to be secure in Him alone. Only then, are we able to gain victory and enjoy relationships the way God intended.

## Getting to Know the Real You

As God weeds out those toxic, unhealthy relationships, learn to talk to Him about how you feel. As you are talking to Him, you are, in return, developing a relationship with Him; and He will begin to speak to you about you. Once you become secure in God and in yourself, it's easier to eliminate people who add no purpose to your life. As I began to desire God more than anything, I went through a lonely period, not lonely meaning the absence of God but lonely meaning alone with God. At first, it was not an easy adjustment. I didn't like just hanging out with God all by myself. I felt it wasn't fair; I wanted to talk on the phone or have lunch with someone. I really felt alone and left out, but I did not want just anyone or anything to compensate my feeling of loneliness.

I began to pray and talk to God about my feelings; and as I talked to Him, He let me know I was exactly where I needed to be. He wanted time to talk to me without distractions. God was building me up spiritually. Eventually, I started to use this time to get more in His Word. In coming to know Him, I came to know myself. As He used this time to tell me what He thought about me and how He wanted to use me, my relationship with Him became really personal. Do not think God is punishing you, when He takes you out of the world in order to spend time with you. This is a privilege and an honor. The All Mighty God wants your undivided attention. I found in His Word that nothing could separate the love he has for me (Romans 8:39).

Once you really experience the love of God, you start to love yourself (the right way). He gave me the confidence I needed in myself and in Him. God is good, and He knows what's best for us. Life is too short to keep people around who have no purpose in your life. I know if I had never gone through the lonely period, there is no way I would be where I am today. I would not have the relationship He desired me to have with Him. My heart goes out to other women; so many of us struggle with being alone, but if we could learn to embrace and appreciate it, more of us would be secure with ourselves and with our spiritual lives.

As life givers, God has wonderful plans in store for us; but we have to be willing to position ourselves to hear from Him. God is trying to speak to us as women; He wants us to know our purpose for life, but we must be willing to stand alone with Him and for Him. By doing so, you will receive a great reward: you will come to know the real you, the women God created you to be. God loves us and knows exactly what we want and need. He is faithful and desires for us to have good things, and healthy relationships are part of it. (Jeremiah 29:11)

I thank God for placing certain people in my life. I have prayer warriors to call when I need prayer, a sister in Christ to call when I need encouragement, and He places me on the hearts of broken people or those just needing prayer. God is faithful. Going through the alone time makes me appreciate my relationships even more, because I know it is God who supplies all of my needs, and I give Him glory! Just spend quality time with the Heavenly Father and get to know the real you.

## Know When to Let Go

Some relationships are harder to let go of than others, especially when it comes to long-term boyfriends and especially baby daddies. I know, because I had to deal with the struggle of being in a relationship and trying to know God. I wrote, briefly, about where I was before marrying my children's father; and believe me, before we got to the "I do," it was a battle. I had to stay in prayer. These are the most difficult relationships to let go because, first of all, if you are not married, living together and having sex, it's a sin, and Satan loves it. He is fighting to win; and if you are not strong enough (mentally), he will win. It's funny, because when we are actually shacking up, (no real woman, honestly, wants to shack up) the enemy is tricking us and robbing us of a real purposeful future and a relationship with God. I don't mean that you don't love God or that God does not love you; but in order for your prayers to prosper, you have to get out of sin. If the both of you happen to be Believers, get married; this gives God something with which to work. Invite God into your home, into your marriage; He will now able to do great things.

1Corinthians 7:9 tells us if you don't have self control, then go ahead and get married; but as long as you are shacking up, the Presence of the Lord is not residing in your home. If it were up to me naturally, I probably would not say this; but because this book is not about me and I am definitely only a yielded vessel, I will say what thus, says the Lord. You can debate it and say that you pray and God forgives, but there is a difference between sinning and living in sin. How do you ask God to forgive you for shacking up and then, continue to shack up? Your prayer should be, "Lord, please provide a way out for me, so I can get out of this life of sin." This gives God permission to move in your life. After this prayer, He will provide a way out for you.

Do not let your boyfriend/baby daddy give you excuses: money, time, fear. Whatever the excuse, do not buy into it, put your foot down, stop giving room to the enemy. If he can live with you, he can marry you. Shacking up is the devil's playground, because we start to depend on the person, not God. You buy a house, purchase cars and start to accumulate things together. Then, when God starts to tug at your heart, trying to draw you closer to Him, you think about the stuff you have together; you wonder how you will make it by yourself. The enemy has you thinking about all of this; and eventually, you take the easy way out, continuing to shack up. God is not glorified in this, because you are not putting your trust in Him. Please, if this is your situation, get out and trust God; and pray for the other individual to come to know God. Pray God softens his heart, because God loves him too. Make a decision not to hinder your spiritual growth any longer by placing other people before God.

## Choosing the Right Friendships

The best way to choose the right friends is to pray and let God add them to your life. As we come to know the person God created us to be, it is critical we associate with others on the same path as us. We have to surround ourselves with others who have a desire to grow spiritually and do more with their lives. Although this walk is definitely possible, it's not always easy. You will have days when you need encouragement; you will need people, in your life, who will support your God given visions and dreams. Only someone secure with himself will be able to sincerely and genuinely be there for you.

Even through my lonely state, I prayed and asked God to place the right people and friendships in my life. He took one relationship to another level, a friendship with my cousin. The bond I share with my cousin is extra special because we're family, and family knows everything about you. This can be good and bad, because regardless of where you are with Christ or how anointed you are, some family members will never feel you; that's okay. We must remember even Jesus was not welcome amongst His own. My cousin and I have definitely had some ups and downs, but God has worked things out for His good. She has been here for me as I write this book. When I'm excited about something God has spoken to me, she is the first person I call. It is very important to have these kinds of spirit filled relationships. Even though you might have to go without for a period of time, God will definitely keep you and fill the void. Most of us have said at some point, "I'm too old to make friends." This is carnal minded talk; we are too old to have long term friendships with no purpose. You can have a new friendship that is more fulfilling than any relationship you've ever had, because it's feeding your spirit and not your flesh.

Married women must understand that just because someone is a friend does not mean she is the person to talk too. We should seek wise counsel about everything. Unless God has actually placed a person on your heart to share with, it's best to keep your marriage business between you and Him or a trusted Godly Pastor. During worship service one day I noticed a new couple; there was something about the wife; I believe my spirit was connecting with her spirit. As time went on, they joined the church; and even though I still had never interacted with her, it was as if my spirit had. After a while, she became my mom's hair stylist, so now I'm thinking, "Okay, Lord, what is it?" Her mother passed away, and I called with my condolences. We would hold small conversations here and there, but that was it. Then, came a time I was really going through some things in my marriage. I had been praying and praying to God and had not talked to anyone besides my Pastor, but I felt I really needed to talk to friend. I told God and he placed her on my heart. At first I was leery about telling my business, but remembered God said for me to call her. I said, "Okay, God, you know her as well as you know me." I called and was so glad I did. She said exactly what I needed to hear; she understood exactly where I was and how I was feeling. This alone caused me to praise God; He knew exactly what I needed. We shared so much with one another in such a short time.

I feel it is important to share this story, because as adult women, we don't experience these kinds of friendships often. You might have a childhood friend or someone you can call anytime who will be there for you. But there is no friendship/relationship more fulfilling than one centered on Christ. As Believers, we cannot make our friends do anything; but it is our responsibility to speak truth to them. We should not condone friendships where there is fornicating, gossiping or anything opposite of a Christian lifestyle. We have to hold one another accountable. We are used to having friends who agree with everything we say and do, and when someone does or says something against how we feel, we immediately get an attitude. As Believers, we have to know it's never about who is right but what's right in any type of relationship.

When you are going through is when you need Godly wisdom and counsel. It doesn't matter how good or nice a person is, how financially stable or how smart; if he does not have a relationship with Christ, the only advice he can give is the wisdom of the world. We have to really evaluate the people we have in our lives; some might stay and some will have to go. Remember, it's always about the quality of your friendships, not the quantity. When you are serious about God and the things of God, wisdom will have you ask Him, "Lord is this friendship pleasing to you?" When He tells you, "No," you must always be willing to let go, because holding on can hold you back. No friendship should be worth loosing the life God has already predestined for you.

## Is it Okay to Date?

I know it can be hard for single women to receive from a married woman; but I have not been married my entire Christian walk. I mentioned earlier I was in a relationship with my children's father and had to make a decision. I could have ignored the Holy Spirit, pretending that we were all ready on the right path, acting as if he was already my husband. Let me give you a revelation from the Lord, either you are a married woman or a single woman. Once I decided to live my life for God, my children's father and I had to go all the way back to the beginning, as if we didn't have a connection. God is a God of decency and order. We were already out of order before living for God; but now, since we were purposing to live for Him, we had to do things in order, regardless of already having children. They were never His plan.

When you have built a successful, mature relationship with God, dating has to be done with purpose, with the intentions of being married. As Believers, we don't date because we are lonely, want sex, or need help with our bills. Even though I married as a baby in Christ, God graced and strengthened me to be able to seek Him before making this step. This is truly when I learned to trust and depend on God. This was a supernatural experience for me, because only God sustained us for almost a year of no sex, when we had been having sex for almost five years without conviction.

During our pre-God years of dating, on several occasions my boyfriend was unfaithful to me, which created a lot of insecurities, low self esteem and distrust in me. I kept taking him back, because I didn't want him to be with anyone else. But, after I started to live for God, I didn't worry about what he was doing or who he was doing it with. I was secure in myself and in God. The new me had given this relationship to God; and I knew if my man slept around before we got married, then it wasn't meant to be. It was just that simple.

It's amazing how we were able to go back to dating. When we are in the world, we fail to take the time to get to know the men we date; we are more excited about just having somebody. In the back of our minds, we are hoping we don't find out anything negative that would cause our antennas to come up; and even when they do, we often ignore the signs. But, God is a revealer; He is the one who reveals, not the devil. As Christian women, we have to represent and glorify God at all times. You might be the closest thing to God a person will ever see. I know it was because I was able to be strong in God and stand in faith, that my husband was able to experience the love of God for himself. I know it pleased God when I invited Him into my decision to marry my husband. It even surprised me, when I came to a place in my heart where I was able to sincerely say, "God, if this is not what You want, then it's not what I want." I meant this when I said it. I believe God want us all to come to a place where we are satisfied with Him alone. When you come to this place, then, I believe, if it's your desire, it is okay to date but only with the intention of the two of you getting married to each other. Until then, learn to fall in love with Jesus; He will never let you down.

## Victory Prayer

Lord, remove everything and every person who is a hindrance to me in my relationship with you. Let every unhealthy relationship fade away and strengthen me to let go and not be regretful. Lord, I only want what you have for me, help me to be secure in you, so I may be secure in myself. I will no longer get caught up in relationships with men who have no intentions of marrying me. Help me to embrace the fact that I might have to spend a lot of time alone with you before even considering dating. Thank you, in advance, for helping me get to a place of true contentment. In Jesus' name, Amen.

## Chapter 5 - Victory in Your Home (Married)

Humanity is lost. We are living in a time where same sex marriages are raising children; and women are purposely having babies out of wedlock, with no intention of getting married. The enemy is using celebrities to promote having babies out of wedlock as being sexy and a personal choice. This is a new trend of the world, not behavior Believers should imitate. We serve a God who does everything decent and in order. Marriage is an institution created by God between a male and a female; but society tells us marriage is whatever you want it to be, with whoever you want. This is so far out of the Will of God. The enemy is trying his best to destroy the marriage institution, because he knows marriage is an institution from God, ordained by God. It is the one and only institution that represents and glorifies God. Godly marriage is how we display the love of God in the natural; and the enemy can't stand it, so, he brings the confusion of same sex marriages, he fills women's heads with lies, telling them they don't have to get married in order to have children. The enemy knows if he can destroy marriages, he can destroy homes and that will destroy children. Destruction always brings death, not always physical death, but spiritual death. From this perspective, we can see why churches are messed up, because homes are out of order. My Pastor says all the time, "Strong families create strong churches."

God is bringing order back into the lives of Believers. We have to stop being defeated by the enemy first, in our personal lives and then, in our homes. It's time Christians step up and speak up, especially women, because we have the ability to change and make things happen. You have to purpose to stop giving room to the enemy and walk in the victory God gave us. Married or single, you have to let the devil know he cannot come and set up camp in your home, on your territory. As wives, we have to fight for victory in our homes. The enemy knows when we are purposely living by the order of God, who will bring deliverance and healing to our homes and, also, to the homes of those watching us. God is all about building his Kingdom and saving souls; the enemy is all about tearing it down. But, to God be the Glory! We have authority over the evil one and power to keep him out of our homes. We have to set the atmosphere, starting with our attitudes. Always, take the time to play praise and worship music; let the Glory of the Lord fill your house. This will send the enemy packing.

## A God of Decency and Order

To have victory in your home, as a married woman, you must know and understand God's order in marriage: God first, husband, wife, and then, children. Many marriages fail because someone did not accept the order of marriage and/or his/her place in the order. I thank God for placing me under a pastor who teaches this order. When you acknowledge God is at the very top, the husband submits to God and the wife submits to the husband; thus, it's so crucial to have a Godly husband. I have spoken to many Believing women married for five plus years who are still defeated. Many couples married before coming to know Jesus Christ; and when there is spiritual imbalance, there is difficulty in the marriage. But, you can still gain the victory in your home and over your marriage. 1Corinthians 7:14 should bring encouragement to the hearts of wives that are praying for their husbands to be saved.

*For the unbelieving husband has been sanctified through his wife...*

So if it's their souls that we are genuinely concerned about, God has already worked it out for us. Now we must continue to pray for their deliverance. And as wives we have the power and authority to stand against the devil on our husbands behalf. Be encouraged and don't allow the enemy to make you feel defeated. Because you have the victory! I call your husband saved, healed, and delivered in Jesus name! Now receive it in your heart.

While I was never caught up on being married, that's not true for the majority of women. I believe they are caught up with the image of marriage, but they don't know anything about the institution itself. Many think marriage is about getting a husband, and then, all needs will be met; but whether married or single, God is the only one who can fulfill your needs. You have to know God in order to build a successful marriage. Society tells us success is gaining fame or wealth, but true success and prosperity come from God. In order for anything to be truly successful, God has to be a part of it.

*Do not let this book of Law depart from your mouth; meditate on it day and night, so that you may be careful to do everything written in it. Then you will be prosperous and successful.* Joshua 1:8

Because warning always comes before destruction, singles, in this generation, will have a greater responsibility to God. God is showing Himself more than ever. He is definitely removing the spirit of ignorance and replacing it with knowledge. God is looking to single Christian women to step up and make the decision not to have babies before marriage. No longer can we use the excuse of being lonely to justify sex before marriage (fornication). A man should not be able to whisper sweet nothings in your ear and you fall for it. God is proving to you He is literally all you need. There is never condemnation when you are a child of God. If you already have children, life may be a little harder, but God is not angry with you. However, if you find yourself years into your Christian walk, continuing to have babies out of wedlock, at some point, you have to ask yourself: "What is really the problem?" God will always meet us at our point of need, when we ask.

Maybe you are trying to fill some type of void or insecurity. You must learn to recognize your weakness and struggles, so God can fix you and make you whole.

*Everyone who drinks this water will be thirsty again, but whoever drinks the water I give him will never thirst.* John 4:13-14

You have to learn to speak life when everything appears dead. You have to learn to be, not only a praying woman, but a praying wife. Pray over your home, marriage and children daily; it is your God given responsibility. Do not give room to the enemy by letting him in to set up camp in your home. Speak life right now, in Jesus name; and the devil will flee. If your marriage is decent and in order, God will heal the situations in your marriage.

## How to Be a Godly Wife

Most women of today tend to have the trophy wife mentality: as long as they look good, smell good, can cook and clean, they are wife material. This worldly mentality is far from the truth. As a Believing wife, you are called to cover your husband in prayer, to assist him in whatever God has called him to do. Of course, you should be physically attractive for him, but it's bigger than just that. The Power of a Praying Wife by Stormie Omartian is a book every woman, married or single, should read. Stormie explains how and what it means to truly pray for your husband, *"First of all, let me make it perfectly clear that the power of a praying wife is not a means to gain control over your husband, so don't get your hopes up! In fact, it is quite the opposite. It's laying down all claim to power in and of yourself and relying on God's power to transform you, your husband, your circumstances, and your marriage."*

As you pray for your husband, you are admitting to God that you have no power to change him, but you know He has all of the power. It wasn't until desperately crying out to God that I began to learn how to pray for my husband; and as I begin to cry out to God about my husband, He began to soften my heart toward him. I began to see my husband the way God sees Him, not the way the enemy wanted me to see him. I experienced just how much God loved my husband and how patient and long-suffering He was toward him.

God started to work on me, and it came as a surprise that I was the one God was really trying to fix. I was the one doing all the praying. I was the one studying His Word. I was the one listening to nothing but praise and worship music. I was the one serving in ministry at our church. So, my question was, "What's wrong with me Lord?" Then, God spoke to my heart and said, "You are the willing one; you have to assist me in getting your husband delivered." He pretty much made it clear that my husband's deliverance, in every area of his life, was tied to my obedience. I thought, and still think, this is craziest thing ever; it makes absolutely no sense to my flesh, and honestly, sometimes it agitates me…a little. So, you can imagine how the enemy will try to fill my head with lies: "You are a fool; he is manipulating you; he will never change; he should be the spiritually mature one; he can't really love you acting like that; it's been this long and he still has not changed."

Because God had already spoken, I now have to call the enemy the liar that he is and walk by faith with what God has already said. Basically, as long as I'm doing what I need to do as a wife, my husband will receive deliverance. When I disobey and give in to the flesh, I could possibly hinder what God wants to do. Unfortunately, because I am human, I have given in many times. Before I learned to truly pray, I was like many other wives, I: nagged, complained, cursed, yelled, cried, and set up counseling sessions. I still have to remain prayerful and purpose not to do these things. So many times, I got out of the Will of God by telling my husband just how much of a screw up he was and how he was hindering our whole family. Have you ever heard the saying, "There are 2 sides to every story?" Actually, there are three sides: your side, the other person's side, and then, there is Truth (God's side). We will never see a situation the way God sees it, unless we pray, and even then, we will not get the entire picture.

The most challenging part of becoming a praying wife is to keep a clean heart before God. This does not mean being perfect; but you must confess your sins daily, being honest with God and giving Him all your feelings toward your husband, the good and bad. You have to allow God to transform you; it is not your responsibility to worry about how or when your husband will be delivered. As you take care of what is precious to God, He will take care of what is precious to you. You, as the wife, have to make a decision to not believe the lies of the enemy; you have to confess daily you will not give up on your husband, you will not turn him over to the enemy, and he will be delivered, healed and changed.

It is important to speak this every day, regardless of how you feel and what the situation looks like. I had to come to a place where I realized that, as a wife, I am called to assist my husband in fulfilling his purpose. This is a big job, and only true love can accomplish it. There were times when I had to put aside my own desires of wanting affection, love and attention, and rely on my God to supply my needs. But, as I obey God, I literally see my husband change right before my eyes. Once we realize God knows everything, we no longer cry selfish prayers of: Lord, change my husband; I need attention; I need affection, I wish my husband would do more.

As you mature as a Believer, you will understand automatically that God knows what you need; and with this confidence, you can pray for one another. God is a jealous God. Everything you can get from another person, God is able to give you, so it's not pleasing to Him when we aren't satisfied with Him. Because I had already shown myself to be faithful to God and had grown to love Him more than anything else, I then, positioned myself to be blessed by my husband. Again, had we first followed the order of God: becoming a Believer, developing a mature relationship with God, getting married, having children, we could have by-passed all the extra heartache. God is able to tell your mate exactly what you need, thus both of you have to be able to hear from God.

So many times I cried out to God during the trials in my marriage, and it always appeared like God favored my husband, even though I knew that wasn't the case. I am speaking to wives who are more spiritually mature than their husbands, not better than or more favored by God; but your faith is more developed. While this is certainly not the Will of God, it is reality. I was always the one who had to apologize or was being convicted by something I had said or done. I would pout, waiting for my husband to apologize when God was telling me to do it. I understand now, that God knew I was secure in His love, and He wanted my husband to experience His love through me. How awesome is our God! This made my spirit sensitive to hear what God was saying about my husband and how He wanted to use me to help him.

I begin to fast and pray; I asked God to show me how and what to pray for my husband. God created us to be bendable and adaptable; you have the ability to secure your husband through your conduct. It's easy to become frustrated and discouraged, when we don't feel our husbands are where they should be spiritually, but as a Believing wife you have to decide that you will love on your husband until you see the manifestation of the victory God has already promised.

*Love is patient, love is kind. It does not envy, it does not boast, it is not proud. [5] It does not dishonor others, it is not self-seeking, it is not easily angered, it keeps no record of wrongs. [6] Love does not delight in evil but rejoices with the truth. [7] It always protects, always trusts, always hopes, always perseveres.* 1Corinthians 13:4-8

As long as your husband is not physically abusive, committing adultery or has abandoned you, God can turn your marriage around; and even if you are going through any of the above, God can still work it out. Pray, seek Godly counsel and use wisdom because every situation is unique. What worked for me may not work for you. Pray and ask God to speak to you about your marriage and situation; believe me, He will.

A successful marriage has nothing to do with your circumstances or your financial status. You can walk in the victory and enjoy your marriage whatever state it's in. As a Believing wife, you must first make up your mind that you will not fall prey to the enemy and end up in divorce court. You must declare you have the victory in your home and in your marriage.

## Raising Godly Children

Regardless of how the child was brought into this world, God has a plan and a purpose for each child. As parents, we have been given stewardship over the children we parent; our children do not belong to us but to God. Children in this generation are so far removed from the plan of God. It all goes back to order; children are only to be born to a husband and wife. While this may not be reality, it is God's best. It's sad to see parents curse their children or act inappropriately toward them; you must realize you are accountable for the damage done toward your children. It is so important to raise your children the right way; God's way. God tells us in His Word to

*Train up a child in the way he should go: and when he is old, he will not depart from it.*
Proverbs 22:6

He is saying, not only tell them what to do, but show them through your own conduct. If you want your children to walk upright before God, you must walk upright before God. Our children have to see us going to church, praying, studying the Word; children are always watching. When we were children, we imitated our parents, the good and bad. It's amazing to me how much we can harm our children without realizing it: with the music we listen to, with our attitudes, what we say around them. This all has an impact on our children. While it's impossible to keep them away from everything, we can limit their exposure. On the other hand, my children go to church, they praise and worship God and they pray; but it's only because they are being taught. They do not automatically know; we have to plant it in them. We are the standard. Our children have to know the difference between a

Christian and the world.

It is our duty to make sure our children's gifts and talents are made manifest. Praying daily for your children and ask God to show you the gifts and talents He has placed inside of them. You cannot live through your children or make them be what you want them to be; God has already uniquely gifted them. While it is true that God knows everything, He doesn't make everything happen, without effort on our part. Because I am the parent of a son with down-syndrome, God has placed on my heart to share with women raising children with special needs. No one is ever really prepared to raise a child with any type of disability, but it happens. When it does, you have to embrace it; it is the right thing to do. Of course, not everyone will take on the responsibility; they will terminate the pregnancy or give the child up for adoption. I know this is not the will of God, no child is an accident.

While carrying my child, the enemy tried to destroy me; I learned during the fourth month there was a possibility my child might be born with down-syndrome. Obviously, it was a hard pill to swallow. Of course, I prayed, even though I was not really living a Christian lifestyle. Toward the end of my pregnancy, I really felt like my baby would be 'normal.' I sighed with relief when he was finally born, because I thought children with down-syndrome had the strong, down-syndrome features; my baby did not appear to have any of these. When he was two days old, I really looked at him and thought to myself, "His features are a little different." Up until that point, no one had said anything about my child having down-syndrome. I asked the nurse, "Did they mention my baby having down-syndrome?" She said she would have the doctor talk to me. He told me that my baby did have features of down-syndrome, and he would have to run tests. At this point, I pretty much knew the answer.

Immediately, the enemy came; my feelings went from a loving mother to someone who did not even want to look at her baby. I cannot explain my flood of emotions; how and why, out of all the people in my family who had healthy children could be happening to me? I was embarrassed for my child and myself, embarrassed for his father, now my husband, for giving him a "less than perfect child." Now, I am embarrassed to even admit to all of this, but it's true. Thank God, I no longer feel this way and haven't for a long time. Only by the grace of God was I able to embrace my baby and pray for his future abilities, gifts and talents. I learned to see the positive side, all the support and most of all, the love my husband showed me and our baby.

God has graced me in so many areas in order to share with the world, so others, too, may be healed and delivered. Once I began to walk as a true Christian, I learned how to pray and cover my children. Amazingly, God speaks to me about my children, showing me exactly how He will use them. My down-syndrome child has helped me in so many areas of my life; he has taught me true love. If I had never come to a place of acceptance, I would have missed a big part of what God has for me. Whether you have a 'normal' child or a child with any kind of physical or mental disability, he is a gift from God; and God doesn't make mistakes.

You have to come to a place of acceptance and thank God for trusting you with His precious gift. He knows He cannot give this precious gift to just anyone. Not everyone chooses to use his God given capability to handle a 'less than perfect' baby; so if God has blessed you with an 'extra special' gift, thank Him. In return, you will be blessed beyond measure. It's not the child who's the extra special gift but God using the child to do something extra special in your life. You must be able to see it this way, or the enemy will make you feel like God has cursed you. Make him out to be the liar he is, and thank God for your gift.

## Victory Prayer

Lord, being a wife is not easy, but I thank You for the institution of marriage. I thank You for the wisdom and knowledge You are pouring into this generation. So many of us never experienced godly mothers; we were not raised in godly homes. We came into our marriages not knowing what to expect, but now, that we know better, we can do better. Show me my place in my marriage; help me to allow my husband to be the leader You created him to be. Lord, I want to be a help, not a hindrance to my husband. Give me patience to be a godly mother, a mother who trains up her children the right way. Lord, I surrender my home to You. In Jesus' name, Amen

## Chapter 6 – Victory in Your Home (Singles)

A single person is one who is unmarried. Unfortunately, in today's world, we have two states of being single: single with no children or single with children; and whether you have children or not, your first obligation is to the Lord. It was never God's plan for there to be single parents, but there are, and there is no condemnation. Where we get off track is trying to factor the child's father into our single state, but God tells us in 1 Corinthians 7:33-34 that an unmarried person is busy with the work of the Lord. I believe God is trying to hold us accountable for our actions.
It is okay to say we messed up; fell in love with the wrong person, every woman has been there. But, at some point, you must take responsibility for your part and keep pushing. Either, you had a child before becoming a Believer or you fell as a Believer. Whatever the situation, as long as you have repented before God, He forgives you; but after forgiveness, you now have to get back into the Will of God.

You can be single and at peace, but only when you are real with yourself. As I observe single women from all age groups, the biggest concern they have is being single. Nobody wants to be 'alone.' They forget God is always with us; we have to learn to be content with God alone. Remember, God is a jealous God. Once you learn to be satisfied with Him, He will send your mate, if that's your desire.

I don't encourage anyone to marry just because of a child. I have been a single Christian; and if I had not had children, I honestly think I could have been very comfortable in the single state. I didn't desire to marry just because of the children, but it was fifty percent of the reason. If you are a single mother, the devil's goal is to distract you and make you discontent; he will try to make you feel guilty for not having a father in the house. But, when you give your situations over to God, He will always work it out for good. God will send men and mentors into your child's life, but you have to believe He can. God is calling us to higher level in our current state: single with or without kids.

## Keeping God First

Every single woman gains victory by learning to keep God first. Since you have no husband, God is your number one priority; Jesus should be your reason for everything. By observing single women, God has shown me that singles are busy trying to occupy their loneliness with other people/things. They say they're happy being single, but their actions show they're really trying to fulfill a lonely void. Because most of their friendships are with other single women, no one in their circle will speak out. They're fooling themselves thinking they are enjoying the single life.

Once we became Christians, we were told by the Word of God to renew our minds. Being a single Christian means you cannot entertain yourself the way the world does. Christians should not desire to go to happy hours or clubs. Many Christian women like to debate this issue; but if you are serious about God and His Kingdom, you will become Kingdom-minded; your only goal/agenda will be to win souls. We are so busy trying to fulfill ourselves, not realizing Christianity is not about us. If you are not able to die to yourself, there is no point in being a Christian. Winning souls is not just preaching, "Jesus is Lord, Confess your sins;" it's a lifestyle. Letting others see your joy is the best way to win unbelievers to Christ; but if you are bored with your walk, how can you convince someone else to join you? Being a Christian is anything but boring. Once you get serious about God and spend time in His Presence, He will reveal to you His plan for your life. This will give you hope and fulfillment; because once

He shows you a vision, it is already done. Your purpose for getting up every day will be to walk out this purpose.

You will learn to fight temptation, because the Holy Spirit will bring to your remembrance the plan God has for your life; and your goal will be not to mess it up. You will purpose everyday to be in the center of His Will. If you live alone, you should never be at home alone with a member of the opposite sex. If you are dating, you should always be together in a public setting. This is wisdom and how God protects our lives. If other women don't respect themselves, Christian women should. We obtain respect by first respecting ourselves. There should be a difference between women who are Believers and women who are unbelievers.

Single Christians have to be cautious in everything they do, including their music. Be very careful and in tune with yourself; if you are feeling lonely, it's not wise to listen to music about making love. Listening to secular music is not our debate; it's not whether it's right or wrong or a sin, it's about wisdom. If you know a particular type of music gets you in the mood, why listen to it? Listen to praise and worship; I guarantee those feelings will leave. Instead, we would rather toy around with those feelings and let the enemy in. The next thing you know you get a phone call (booty call); then, Sunday you are at the altar crying for forgiveness.

The single state is the only state in which you can freely worship God, freely serve Him and be freely available to Him. If you truly love God, this should excite you. Singles, please stop giving room to the enemy and listening to his lies: "You will never have a man. You are thirty and still single." Give God praise for your freedom! Desiring to be married is okay; but until then, focus on your career and dreams. Take this time to truly love yourself, and you will position yourself for the right one to find you. You do have the Victory over your single state!

## Don't Compromise

To compromise means to expose to danger or difficulty, as by carelessness. For example, as a single Believer who's bored, you decide to receive some male company. You tell yourself it's harmless, but you're giving room to the enemy and exposing yourself to danger. Your carelessness could possibly compromise your relationship with God. The first time brings about some innocent fun which leads you to believe there could be a next time. The next time becomes more physical than the first. The cycle continues and each time brings you closer and closer to your fall. The same thing occurs with being around those who drink or go to the clubs. The first time you might not have a drink; but eventually, you will join in on the fun.

The enemy always begins very subtly; and then takes you down when you were least expecting it. He wants us to compromise our fellowship with God, leading the way to condemnation. If you are not feeding on the Word of God, condemnation can pull you right back in to the world. Being a baby in Christ, is not the time to prove how strong you are to other people. Say, "No," to the flesh and drawing closer to God is the beginning of Christian maturity. Struggles of the flesh will always be present; but a mature Christian is not struggling with going to clubs, drinking or sexual sins. At some point, we have to get past these things in order for God to be able to trust and use us. God understands our temptations, so he gives us more grace and mercy to deal with them. Every time we say, "No," to the flesh, we position ourselves to be blessed.

In the beginning of my walk with God, after I decided to live for Him, I always found myself caught between a rock and hard place. My friends and family were not used to the new me, so they automatically expected me to do things I did before. You will still be invited to parties/clubs, and your flesh will want to say, "Yes," because you don't want anyone to think you are different, when in reality, you are. You have to decide: do you compromise your fellowship with God and please man, or do you follow the Spirit and position yourself for a blessing?

Friends invited me to their birthday parties, and either the party would be in a night club or at their home in an environment I knew would include smoking marijuana and drinking. Each time I kindly refused, trying not to be condemning, but letting them know I didn't do those things anymore. There were times I cried out to God, because I didn't want to be different; but I still said, "No," and with each "No," He would give me more grace. Eventually, no one bothered to ask me anymore; they would respectfully say, "I'm having a party; I didn't bother inviting you because I knew you wouldn't want to come," and they would invite me to lunch or something more appropriate for me. I believe people love to see someone stand firm in her beliefs, because, especially women, we all want to live in victory, even though your victory might be different from mine. We want to see it is possible to be the real woman God created us to be; and the real woman God created you to be does not compromise for other people but stands firm in her beliefs.

## Raising Children Alone

Today, we see lots of single women raising children and hear negative comments about children coming from single parent homes. We are aware of those doing a poor job, but I personally know and admire plenty of single Christian women their raising children alone. I have seen the faithfulness of God in the lives of these single women and their children. Whether you had a child living a life of sin, you are divorced, widowed, or forced to raise someone else's children, God is faithful. Once you give your life over to Him, He will take care of you, your children and your children's children. God is a father to the fatherless; He is whatever you need Him to be. As a single parent with little or no help from the father, all you can do is your part and let God handle the rest.

One of the best decisions a mother can make for herself and her children is to join a God ordained church. Your child/children need to be part of a church with a Child Care Ministry to meet their spiritual needs. If you do not have a church home, pray and ask God to lead you to one; He will. Many Christians wait for things to happen; but we must pray; and after we pray, we should listen to the voice of the Lord and follow His instructions. Because of my children, I was motivated to do something different with my life; it's not enough to say you love your child, love moves you into action. Once you decide to involve your children in a church, you will be blessed beyond measure.

God uses babies and small children. I'm sure you have experienced your child saying exactly what you needed to hear at a certain moment; it made you do a double take. It blesses me that my children have a church home and are being taught the Word of God. Children see enough of the world at school, in stores and restaurants; they have to know there is a right way, God's way, to live. They have to be taught what is right and what is wrong. I know they will make mistakes, but they have to learn early in life that God's Spirit dwells on the inside of them, and He speaks in a still quiet voice. My children are five and six; we joined our church when they were one and two, and I thank God for their knowledge of God and Jesus at this early age. The first sentence my five year old said was, "Thank you, Jesus," with his hands raised! I know, had he not been exposed to this expression of thankfulness, his first words could have been anything but godly.

Most children will grow up knowing and doing what they are around, whatever is familiar; but when we are purposing to be in the center of God's will, He will always provide. God will place father figures, role models and mentors in your children's paths. He will not let your child lack any good thing, when you are faithful to him. You do not have to have a boyfriend in order for your child to have a father figure. You must stay faithful to God; let your children see you being faithful, and they will follow your example. God makes provisions for us. Do not let the enemy tell you, you cannot raise a successful child as a single parent, because with God anything is possible. You and your child have the Victory!

## Victory Prayer

Heavenly Father, help me to embrace my single state. I will no longer compromise my relationship with You; I will keep You first in my life.

I trust You to help me raise god fearing children. Thank You for sending role models and mentors into their lives to teach them what I can't.

Thank You for victory in my home and for your protection. Most of all, thank You for forgiveness. In Jesus' name, Amen

## Chapter 7- Victory on Your Job

If we can all grab hold of the fact that life is one big test, I believe we can start to live differently and make better decisions. Being a Christian is not only for church and ministry; it's who you are no matter where you are. Christianity is a lifestyle; it's saying to God, "Lord, use me!" For many of us, our work place holds the biggest challenges, because at work, we are around people with different backgrounds, cultures, beliefs, morals and lifestyles. It's not like church, or like those with whom you choose to fellowship. While you would think most of us Believers would take this as an opportunity to glorify God, instead we complain about being the only Christian. Before I re-dedicated my life back to Christ, I was at a job where nearly everyone claimed to be a Christian. Most of them went to church every Sunday, a couple of them were in their church choir, one carried her Bible to work every day and read it on her lunch break. But even with all of this, there was no evidence of their lives being truly changed. They still cussed, fornicated, smoked cigarettes and practiced other worldly behaviors. I'm not judging their Christianity, but they did not compel me to want God. I do thank Him though, for His grace and mercy which allowed me to know, as a Christian, I did not want to be like them.

When I first started this job, I was not in church and had not been for a while; now, I know God placed me there for a reason. After working there for eight months, one Sunday, I gave my life back to Christ. When I returned to work the following week, I was a 'new creature' and excited about Jesus! Of course, my co-workers were excited for me; but as I continued going to church and learning more about being a Christian, I believe conviction came upon them. After growing more in Christ, I hated going to work. I hated the type of Christians they were, so I began showing up, as many Believers do, with a 'holier than thou' attitude. I began to separate myself from them.

It's funny to think about now, but I guess I thought I was standing up for Christianity. I am so grateful that God is all knowing; He knows what is inside our hearts and what makes us act the way we do. This is never an excuse to sin; but if you truly mean well, God will expose your behavior to you, cause you to repent and to change that behavior! I cried out to God, "Lord, please give me another job." It was after this prayer that God spoke to and began to deal with me about my attitude. He told me I was at this job for a reason and that I needed to display a Christian to my co-workers. As soon as He spoke this, I received it. Instead of complaining, on the way to work, about my co-workers, I started to pray for them; and listening to my praise and worship music on the way changed me drastically; I no longer judged them. I began to minister in love; and in return, they began to receive. God is awesome, when we obey His voice. After I allowed God to use me, my co-workers witnessed Him elevate me to a new place of employment.

*Therefore humble yourselves [demote, lower yourselves in your own estimation] under the mighty hand of God, that in due time He may exalt you.* 1 Peter 5:6

If you are the only one at your job who is purposing to live like Christ, then you must understand you are on an assignment. You may never know who's watching you or whose life you may impact, but God has you there to sow a seed. Your assignment may not be easy, and you may not act exactly as God intended; but God is also building godly character in you. Learn from your mistakes and keep a repentant heart. Our job is to imitate Christ; we must know we are the light God has sent into the dark places, so praise Him for sending you.

This is not the time to complain that you are the only Christian; this is the time for Kingdom business. Christianity is about saving souls; people are not only saved by someone preaching to them. Someone, who has never experienced genuine love, can be saved by our show of Christian love. Most people in the world have never experienced a true Christian. We must allow God to use us to show the world Christianity is real. God's grace is sufficient for the task, so allow Him to use you.

## Respecting Authority

Gaining victory at work starts with respecting authority. When we respect authority, we glorify God. It took me thirty years to grasp this, and there are forty, fifty and sixty year olds who still do not understand respecting authority. We feel if we are grown, then we are the authority. Many people lose jobs, because authority told them to do something they did not like. I quit many jobs because I did not like who the authority was or how they treated me. Authority was created by God for our protection. Authority has nothing to do with the person; it's the position that must be respected.

God allowed me to go through a situation at work, when he placed a person living a gay lifestyle in a role of authority. I am not homophobic, but I believe what God says in His Word about sexuality. Although my spirit was bothered and uncomfortable, I still had to respect her and the position. This was not the time to talk about my disapproval of the lifestyle of this person with authority over me. God does not hate people; He hates sin. I did express my share of murmuring and complaining, until God convicted me. Once I mastered this struggle, this same person in authority replaced our regular prayer ritual with meditation, because it was 'less offensive.' Again, I was crying to God, "Lord, Lord, what's going on?"

One Sunday, I shared my concerns with a few women in the Spiritual Counseling Ministry to which I belong. We prayed. I held on to this wise remark from one of the women, "It's okay that she removed prayer, but you can still pray." I love these strong women of God! Once again, God graced me to gain victory over the enemy. The devil wanted to pull me from under God's umbrella of protection through gossiping, fear, discouragement, and other behaviors not glorifying to God. As Believers, we must learn to pray through adverse situations and let God move on our behalf. You cannot pray acceptably and get results, when you are operating in disobedience; and not respecting authority is disobedience. Do not allow authority to abuse, misuse and disrespect you; let God fight the battle. He can work it out like no one can.

I am sure that victory was won; what the devil meant for harm, God used for His glory. This boss was promoted to another position, yes promoted. It is not God's Will for anybody to be fired, even though it can happen. Your prayer should never be, "Lord, fire her; cause her to lose her job." This is not a godly prayer. Remember, whether you serve God or the world, they both give promotions. God was so amazing! Before my supervisor's promotion, God arranged for us to have a one on one conversation and used me to demonstrate the love He had for her. Both of us sat tearfully in her office as God gave me the right words to say. Praise His Name!

During our childhood, we were required and expected to respect authority, but many of today today's youth do not. I blame their parents as poor examples; how can we teach our children to obey if we don't? God demands accountability. He is bringing order back into the lives of His people to be witnesses to those watching us, especially in the workplace, one of the largest environments, outside of the church, where we are held accountable. How you act and react at your place of employment will show God what you learned from the messages at Sunday Services and Bible Studies. We come to church to hear from God and receive the power to tell the world about Jesus through our conduct and attitude. If you are facing a challenging situation at work, evaluate it; make sure you are in line with God in order to be in a right place to receive your promotion.

# God - the True Source

As Believers, we must know God is our Source; He is the Source that brings resources. It's not about our job or title, our educational level, our financial status; God placed the gifts and talents on the inside of us. He is in control of our learning abilities, ambitions, our drive to succeed; God is the One who makes everything possible. We would be foolish to think we have obtained degrees, jobs and other accomplishments all on our own. God understands education and knowledge are power, but His Wisdom is a necessary ingredient to our level of education. A person with knowledge/education and degrees but no Godly Wisdom is a dangerous person. On the flip side, a person with no education and degrees but possesses Godly Wisdom is blessed, because God's Wisdom will bring creativity and opportunities; it will open doors and bring resources.

A person possessing Godly Wisdom is thinking about the Kingdom and how to use this Wisdom to be a blessing to others. Those who have achieved on their own, without God in the midst cannot understand why they would need Him. They believe they have achieved on their own; and therefore, they do not need anyone. If you are educated, you probably make decent money; and this confuses a lot of people. In this world, we equate money with blessings; if a person has things and money, he is blessed. You do not have to be a Believer in order to get stuff; money can buy you anything material. But, it cannot buy Salvation, healing, deliverance, peace of mind, joy, the return of your lost child; thus, where's its power?

Many times, it takes a desperate situation in the life of a person with wealth and intellect to move him/her to come to God. God tells us in His Word it is difficult for the rich to come into the Kingdom (Matthew 19:24). In spite of all their money, we observe many Hollywood personalities living miserable, sinful lives. Yet, still we Believers try to find satisfaction in money. We look for jobs based on salary and fail to truly trust in God as our Source to the point where money is no object. We should desire to be where

God wants us, even if it means a $5.00 an hour cut in pay. God is Jehovah Jireh (Provider). It is time for us, women of God, to renew our minds.

It is God's desire for us to live in abundance, but He is preparing us for His blessings so we will not be governed by the world's beliefs. God's blessings make us rich and add no sorrow (Proverbs 10:22). As Believers, we are to be Kingdom-minded: we want God to bless us so we can be a blessing to others. If this is not your number one reason for desiring to be blessed, then you've missed it! God knows we want money for our children's college fund, a bigger house, a nicer car, a fine vacation; He understands! But, He tells us to take care of what's precious to Him and He will take care of what's precious to us (Luke 12:24). God is all about building His Kingdom and winning souls.

As women of God, we should look to God for promotions, not man (employer or self); and whatever we do, do it as unto the Lord (Colossians 3:23-24). We have to work our jobs as if we report directly to God, Himself. Working this way will cause doors of opportunity to open, because we are not trying to please people. Trying to please man only moves us into sin, because we are relying on an individual to promote us, instead of God. If we only knew how big His promotions are! If you are looking for a job or in a job you're not sure of, take time to seek the face of God and ask Him if you are in the center of His Will. Allow Him to direct you; there is no greater fulfillment than being in God's Will. Trust in Him; allow Him to use you so others will ask about the God you serve.

## God - the True Rewarder

I sense, in my spirit, God is telling us, women of God, to learn to trust Him with our whole hearts. God wants us to live in abundance and the overflow of His goodness. He is not glorified when we are broke or have dreams but no resources to fulfill those dreams. It is God's desire for His children to prosper. Do we really believe God can provide for us more than our paychecks? It honors God when we trust and rely on Him. Faith moves the hands of God, believing He will reward us according to His riches (Philippians 4:19). When we fully understand we work for God and not man, when we learn to do everything we do as unto the Lord, He will reward us, His children. I beg of you to make sure your security is not in your job or bank account. If it is God will take it all away just so that you will know He is the one in control of everything that we have, including our jobs. And He is the True source.

## Victory Prayer

Lord I come to you with a repentant heart, if I have been out of line or not respecting authority I ask you to show me. Help me to understand that it's not about the person but the position. When I disrespect those who have charge over me it is really you I am disrespecting. If my trust is in my job, bank account, or savings show me and help me to trust and see you as my source. In Jesus' name. Amen.

## Chapter 8 - Victory over Your Finances

If you are like me, you came into the Kingdom with no money and/or bad credit. Now, you're trying to figure out how to live this Christian lifestyle with the spirit of lack and debt chasing you. First, you love God, not for what you have or need, you love Him for what He has already done for you. Once you give your life to God, the enemy bombards your mind daily with what you don't have: a big house, a new car, expensive clothes, designer shoes, all material things. We have these things, just not the brand name, the extravagance the world looks at. God's Word tells us not to worry about these things (Matthew 6:33). The most important way to gain victory over your finances is to seek the face of God, not His hands (what He can do for us). Seeking God's face gives us wisdom and understanding. God gives the power to gain wealth, but we must understand how we got into financial debt and that we need Godly wisdom to get out. God is not into debt cancellation (although He can); He wants us to learn from past financial mistakes.

In the world, we did whatever we wanted to do with our money. I was careless with money, which is crazy, because I was not taught that at home. My parents always paid their bills and took pride in their credit scores. I picked up a lot of worldly behavior, simply by being around other people living in survival mode. I acquired that 'just trying to survive' mindset. I moved out of my parents' house at eighteen and began accumulating bills; at the same time, I wanted to go to clubs, buy new clothes and take trips out of town. These things were most important to me; the bills got paid whenever. When we are young, we don't realize how much we are influenced by the company we keep. As we get older, we measure our success by material possessions. It's okay to want things, but be careful to monitor your motives to buy something. Is it because someone else has it? Can you afford it?

Any and every thing we have should glorify God. When we purchase things we can't afford: house, car, clothes saying, "God blessed me," but know it isn't in our budget, we usually end up losing what we'd said was God's 'blessing.' This makes either us or God a liar, because God doesn't give us things to take them away. We need to stop referring to things we can afford to buy because of our salaries as God's blessings, because really, we are blessing ourselves. We should thank God for providing a job and the means, but God's blessings are rich and add no sorrow (Proverbs 10:22). To truly experience a blessing from God, we have to be walking in obedience to Him.

## Learning to Give

Saying God has blessed us, means we have been walking in obedience to His instructions and giving to others as He leads us. Giving is not all about money. We can give a word, our time, our talents; but we must reject the mindset of wanting something in return. Give, as being led by God; then, allow Him to pay as He sees fit. I thank God for speaking a word I will always remember, "As I elevate you, never put a price on yourself." This explains how many preaching the Gospel get caught up in the flesh. When we are invited to share our God-given gift(s) of singing, speaking, writing, we set a price for our service; if that price is not met, we refuse. This is not Godly Wisdom, because the Gospel is free.

We should be happy and willing to offer the gifts God has given us without the expectation of personal gain. Many of us pray to be free from the spirit of debt and lack, not living from paycheck to paycheck; first, we must learn to give of ourselves. If you have the time to babysit a struggling mother's child; if you can transport someone who has no transportation to work or school; if you believe God has given you a word to speak to someone; these are all part of giving. When given with the right heart and motive, God will bless you, as you bless the person receiving from you.

It is important to give without murmuring and complaining. "We give for two reasons: out of love and because we are led by God," Pastor Raymond Horry, my Pastor. Giving for one of these goals causes no motivation to complain. Complaining hinders and can stop our blessings. God is maturing us. He knows as we grow spiritually, we will grow financially; but first, seek spiritual maturity. What good is it for a foolish baby Christian to have money? Our approach should be focused on building up God's Kingdom, not our desires of the flesh. If we don't mature, we could cause God's blessings to spoil us.

As Believers, we learn to stand on the Word of God and believe He takes care of His children. God doesn't want us to struggle any more than we want to. Unpaid bills and disconnection notices are not pleasing to God, and worrying about it does not move the hand of God. Instead, start freely giving to others of: your time, your gifts, your talents so God can bless you. Let's break every financial stronghold and defeat the enemy. We are prosperous women of God!

## A Servant's Heart

As unbelievers and living for the world, we sought to serve our own selfish desires. Everything was all about us; we had selfish hearts. We walked in the characteristics of our father, the devil. Selfishness is not a spirit of God. The Lord Jesus Christ came to the earth realm, not to be served or to cater to His own desires; He came to serve the people. He came so we may have hope, healing and deliverance. Jesus was focused on only one mission: to do the will of the Father. Believers have this same calling on their lives. We are followers of Christ; we are to imitate everything He did when He was on earth. Before I came to really know God, I thought everything was about education, a career, being successful. If you are not using your knowledge and skills for the Kingdom, it's all in vain. You can have all the degrees in the world and still lose your soul. God is not impressed with education; He is impressed when we use education for His Glory.

The enemy is clever; he tells us not furthering our education makes us losers, unworthy, causing us to live in survival mode, doing whatever to get by. My spirit says, "God wants to free someone right now!" It's difficult for me to remember walking into stores and taking what I wanted with no conviction, simply trying to make myself look good on the outside. I thank God I was never caught and put in jail. This was not the real me! Whatever ungodly, worldly thing you're doing, this is not the real you. The enemy was tricking me, and he's tricking you. Stealing name brand clothes was my cover up; it helped me portray the image that everything was good. I thank God, daily and say, "Yes" to Him, because I could be dead or in prison. Being broke will never get me to turn my back on God. I urge you to turn to God.

After confessing my past sins to God and believing He would work all things out for my good (Romans 8:28), I feel a sense of freedom and contentment. I no longer want to steal, write bad checks, lie on my taxes or to anyone; this is not God's best. If you are struggling financially, you may have to go without some things and possibly, have to experience disconnections. We must no longer give false account information to keep the lights on and then, call it a blessing. This does not glorify God and will block His working in our lives. First, learn to be content without. God does not intend for us to live without, but He wants us delivered from former behaviors and previous ways of thinking.

Let God do a work in you and make a decision to never give up. As you pray for God to deliver you financially, He, not only will, but will also, enable you to obtain finances. He will, in return for your obedience, change your heart and attitude toward money. When you are sincere, He will prepare you for wealth. He will give you the desires to give, to serve and to tithe which will add increase to His Kingdom. God will add to our finances to accomplish what He has called us to achieve. When living for God, our finances are no longer our own. God understands we need money to live, but a true Believer desires money to be a blessing to others. It's time we all become servants, serving others less fortunate than ourselves, refusing to be selfish. We must serve as Christ did on earth. When we develop this type of attitude, then, God can trust us with true wealth and prosperity.

## We Owe the Tithe

If you came into the body of Christ struggling with finances, chances are after becoming a Believer, you will struggle with tithes and offerings. Don't be hard too on yourself at first; you will soon realize using the excuse, "I'm too broke to tithe," is not acceptable to God. Early in my Christian walk, I wanted to tithe only because I knew it was the right thing to do, but I figured God knew I was barely making ends meet without tithing. For the longest time, I was sure God didn't mind my not tithing until I had extra, over my expenses. Then, I heard Him say to me, "There is no excuse for you not to pay your tithes; you owe the tithe."

For the first time, I felt convicted about not tithing. I cried, I repented, and I took it to the alter many times. It still did not come easy; I confessed to God everyday that I was robbing Him, but I still thought I didn't have enough money to tithe. I finally made up my mind to step out and tithe with my next check; I was so excited, but my check was less than I had expected. I kept my word and tithed anyway, and God graced me to become more faithful. Even though my check was short, it felt so good to tithe.

I realized tithing is a heart thing; it's the love we have for God that compels us to tithe. We realize how grateful we are to God for providing us a church home and a pastor; then, we realize the church and the pastor need money in order to be effective. No person can force us to tithe or make us feel bad about tithing. We have to believe that God wants us to tithe for our own benefit; then, God will give us the desire to tithe. Some people are faithful tithers but their heart is not in it; these tithers are no better than those who don't tithe. We should feel good when we tithe; it shouldn't be a sad or grievous action, but happy and cheerful obedience to God.

You may be as I was, an off and on tither. God revealed to me that I trusted Him in a lot of areas but not with my finances. I confessed, repented and began trusting Him in this area too. Personally, it's still hard; but I do not want to rob God, and when we do not give Him, His ten percent, we are robbing Him. Tithing has always been a sensitive subject among Believers; but giving God ten percent of our income is the least we can do to show Him appreciation for saving us, for providing jobs and resources, for looking after us. God does not need a dime from us, but in order to do His will on earth, He has to use people. God blesses us to be a blessing. When we give God what we owe Him, He is pleased; and in return, He will continue to provide increases, because He knows He can trust us to glorify Him in our giving. Everything boils down to glorifying God so we can pull others into the Kingdom. Make a commitment to give God what is due; He is worth, at least, a dime.

## What About The 90%?

Even though we owe the tithe, it doesn't mean we can do whatever we want with the ninety percent. It's God's desire that we live without lack; but as long as we keep doing whatever we want with our finances, we will never really see God move. We must ask God to direct us in handling the ninety percent. The blessings are amazing, when we take time to consult Him on everything in our lives. Instead of going to the mall after tithing and paying bills, we should ask if He wants us to go.

This might sound a bit radical to you; but understand just who God is, He is in total control. He knows every thought you have: the outfit you want, where to find it, the price and when it will go on sale. If we take time to acknowledge Him, He will tell us, "No, not this week. Be a blessing to Sister or Brother Jones and go to the mall next week." This is far from what we want to hear, so we rebuke Satan and head to the mall anyway. The first thing we see is exactly what we were hoping to find, so we think "This has got to be God," even though, it's over priced. The very next week, we see the same outfit on sale, and what we thought was a blessing, we now regret buying. If we really want to see God move in our finances, we have to acknowledge Him before we spend a dime. Of course, this is not an overnight process; but God honors every step we make, especially with a right heart.

God is calling us, Believing women who claim to know Him, to a higher standard this year. It's time to wake up and listen to God; there's no time for games and playing church. God is about to do a Quick Work, and I am ever so grateful that He had me in mind. His Word tells us,

*...the day you hear His voice, harden not your heart. To them that has ears let them hear what the spirit of the Lord is saying.* Hebrews 3:15

Can you hear His voice? If so, thank Him, praise Him, give Him glory and honor. Make today the day of moving forward; do not look back. We are not perfect, none of us. Therefore, God sent His Son to die for our sins; and when He ascended back to our Father, He left us a Helper, the Holy Spirit. No one can walk this journey alone; but God promised He will never leave nor forsake us. Maybe you have lost someone on whom you depended: a mother, father, grandparent, husband, boyfriend, friend or child. These people are not promised to always be here; but God is always here, and He is faithful.

*He is the same yesterday, today and forever.* Hebrews 13:8

Make a new commitment to God and give Him all of you, no matter the cost. You will have no regrets. You have the Victory. Now, walk in it.

## Victory Prayer

It is you, Lord, who has the power to give wealth and take it away. I understand you are looking for children to be obedient in their giving to You, in order to build Your Kingdom here on earth. Show me how to be a good steward over my money. I have wasted too much of what you have already given me on useless, material things. Now, Lord, I want to be used by You in the area of my finances. Help me to be a faithful tither, so I will not continue to rob You of what is already Yours. Lord, help me to give above and beyond the ten percent tithe. Father, bless me with the attitude of a servant, so I may serve You and Your people more and more. Lord, have your way in me and through me, in Jesus' name. Amen.

## ABOUT THE AUTHOR

Samone Yancy resides in St. Louis, Missouri with her husband and children. She gave birth to Samone Yancy Ministries in October 2012. SYM is called to equip and empower ALL women and to share the love of Christ to those that are lost.. SYM is a one stop shop for women and their families, offering a variety of services and resources, support groups, clothing and food assistance, mentoring, women advocates, community outreach, and more. To know more about SYM or to become a partner or volunteer visit SamoneYancyMinistries.org or contact 314-222-7047.

Made in the USA
San Bernardino, CA
27 September 2015